## Que® Quick Reference Series

# QuickBASIC  Quick Reference

John R. Ottensmann

Que Corporation
Carmel, Indiana

Library of Congress Catalog Number: 88-61933

ISBN 0-88022-373-1

91  90  89  88              4 3 2

Interpretation of the printing code: the rightmost
double-digit number is the year of the book's printing;
the rightmost single-digit number, the number of the
book's printing. For example, a printing code of 88-4
shows that the fourth printing of the book occurred in
1988.

This book is based on Microsoft QuickBASIC version
4.0, the Overlay Linker version 3.61, and the Library
Manager version 3.08.

# Que Quick Reference Series

The *Que Quick Reference Series* is a portable resource of essential microcomputer knowledge. Whether you are a new or experienced user, you can rely on the high-quality information contained in these convenient guides.

Drawing on the experience of many of Que's best-selling authors, the *Que Quick Reference Series* helps you easily access important program information. Now it's easy to look up programming information for C and QuickBASIC 4, as well as often-used commands and functions for 1-2-3, WordPerfect 5, MS-DOS, and dBASE IV.

Use the *Que Quick Reference Series* as a compact alternative to confusing and complicated traditional documentation.

The *Que Quick Reference Series* also includes these titles:

> *C Quick Reference*
> *MS-DOS Quick Reference*
> *1-2-3 Quick Reference*
> *WordPerfect Quick Reference*

**Publishing Manager**
Allen L. Wyatt, Sr.

**Product Director**
Karen A. Bluestein

**Editors**
Gregory S. Croy
Gail S. Burlakoff
Terrie Solomon

**Editorial Assistant**
Ann Taylor

**Technical Editor**
Gordon Arbuthnot

**Trademark Acknowledgments**
Que Corporation has made every effort to supply
trademark information about company names,
products, and services mentioned in this book.
Trademarks indicated below were derived from
various sources. Que Corporation cannot attest to the
accuracy of this information.

IBM is a registered trademark of International
Business Machines Corporation.

Microsoft QuickBASIC is a registered trademark of
Microsoft Corporation.

CodeView is a trademark of Microsoft Corporation.

WordStar is a registered trademark of MicroPro
International Corporation.

# Table of Contents

# Introduction

This quick reference, a compact but complete guide to using Microsoft®'s QuickBASIC 4, is organized into sections that address QuickBASIC programming issues. When you have a question about QuickBASIC, you can turn to the appropriate section for the information you need.

## *Notational Conventions*

The following conventions are used in this quick reference.

Menu commands and commands and options entered at the DOS prompt are displayed boldface in blue, as in:

Select the **Start** command ... or ... enter **bc /d**.

Key names are displayed with initial capital letters:

Press function key F4, and then press Enter.

Syntax lines and sample program lines are displayed in blue in a monospace font. QuickBASIC keywords (whether in blue or not) are displayed in all capital letters, as in:

```
ON ERROR GOTO ErrorRoutine
```

Information to be included by the user within a BASIC statement or function is presented in italics, as in

```
LET var = expr
```

where the value of the *expression* is assigned to the *variable*. Some of the elements most frequently used with BASIC statements or functions are

| | |
|---|---|
| *var* | Any BASIC variable |
| *numvar* | A numeric variable |
| *strvar* | A string variable |
| *expr* | Any BASIC expression |
| *numexpr* | A numeric expression |

| *strexpr* | A string expression |
| *file* | A file or device name, including an optional path |
| *filenum* | The file number used with the OPEN statement |
| *n* | A specific numeric value |
| *type* | A QuickBASIC data type |
| *lineident* | A line identifier (line number or label) |

The meanings of the abbreviated italicized elements in a syntax description are always provided in the explanation of the statement or function.

Within the syntax descriptions of BASIC statements, elements enclosed by square brackets are optional. For example, the syntax of the assignment statement is

```
[LET] var = expr
```

This means that either of the following forms is acceptable:

```
LET var = expr or var = expr
```

When syntax elements are enclosed by braces and separated by vertical lines, you must choose between those elements. For example, the syntax description

```
TIMER {ON | OFF | STOP}
```

means that all of the following are correct BASIC statements:

```
TIMER ON or TIMER OFF or TIMER STOP
```

Three periods following a syntax element indicate that the element may be repeated as many times as necessary. For example:

```
ON expr GOTO lineident [, lineident] . . .
```

means that the final element (a *line identifier* preceded by a comma) may be repeated as many times as necessary. Thus, the following statement is acceptable:

```
ON TestValue GOTO 200, 300, 400, 500
```

Explanations of any other aspects of the syntax descriptions are included in the discussion following the syntax description.

# Using the QuickBASIC Environment

In the QuickBASIC environment, you can enter and edit BASIC programs and debug and run them. To perform these actions, you use commands from pull-down menus, a variety of special keys and key combinations, and (optionally) a mouse.

Start QuickBASIC by entering the command **qb** (followed by any invocation options) at the DOS prompt.

## *Invocation Options*

When you start QuickBASIC, you may enter the following options after the **qb** command:

| | |
|---|---|
| /ah | Used to allow individual dynamic arrays to exceed 64K |
| /b | Used to force monochrome display with a CGA |
| /c:*buffersize* | Used to set buffer size for communications port |
| /cmd *string* | Used to store *string* used by the COMMAND$ function. This option must be the last option entered. |
| /g | Used to force fast screen update. This option may cause "snow" with the CGA. |
| /h | Used to force maximum possible display resolution |
| /l [*libraryname*] | Used to load default Quick Library or the library specified by *libraryname* |

| /mbf | Used to force conversion functions to treat numbers as Microsoft Binary Format numbers |
| /run *sourcefile* | Used to load and run *sourcefile* |
| *sourcefile* | Used to load *sourcefile* |

# Environment Menu Commands

To select a command from the keyboard:

1. Press Alt to move cursor to command line.

2. Display a pull-down menu by pressing first letter of menu topic or by using arrow keys to highlight menu topic and pressing Enter.

3. Select a command from a pull-down menu by pressing highlighted letter of menu command or by using arrow keys to highlight desired command and pressing Enter.

Press the Esc key to cancel or "back out" of commands any time before you execute them.

To select a command with the mouse:

1. Display a pull-down menu by pointing with mouse to menu topic on menu bar and clicking mouse's left button.

2. Select a command from pull-down menu by pointing with mouse to desired command and clicking button.

You may also select some menu commands by using the shortcut keys listed on pull-down menus and in the following command descriptions.

Many menus display dialog boxes that request additional information. To respond to a dialog box:

❏ Move the input focus (highlighted area) by pressing the Tab key.

❑ Move input focus and toggle the option on or off by pressing highlighted letter of item. If using a mouse, point to item and click left button.

❑ Toggle option on or off for highlighted item by pressing space bar.

❑ Cycle through selections by pressing arrow keys.

❑ To accept settings, select OK button and press either Enter or space bar. If using a mouse, point to OK and click left button.

❑ If using a mouse, toggle on or off any option and continue with the command's operation by pointing to item and double-clicking left button.

The following descriptions are of commands in the QuickBASIC environment's various menus. For those commands that have a shortcut key, the key is indicated next to the command's name.

# File Menu

The File menu's commands include the following:

### New Program

Erases any program currently in memory. Use this command to begin a new program.

### Open Program

Erases any program in memory and loads one from disk, including all associated include files and modules. You may specify the program's name by either typing or selecting it.

### Merge

Loads contents of specified disk file into memory, inserting the contents at the cursor's position. Select files as you do with **Open Program** command.

### Save

Saves to disk the current program module.

### Save As

Saves to disk the current program module. You have the option of specifying a new file name and changing the format in which the program is saved.

### Save All

Saves to disk all modules that you have changed since you last saved your work.

### Create File

Begins a new file. You can specify whether the file is to be a module, an include file, or a document.

### Load File

Loads a file from disk. You can specify whether file is to be loaded as a module, an include file, or a document. This command can be used to add a module from another program to the program currently in memory. Loading a file as a document allows an ASCII file to be edited without BASIC syntax checking. Select files as you do with **Open Program** command.

### Unload File

Removes a module from program and from memory. Original file remains on disk. QuickBASIC does not save any changes made to module.

### Print

Prints selected text, the active window, the current module, or all modules.

### DOS Shell

Temporarily exits to DOS so that you can execute other programs and DOS commands. Requires access to COMMAND.COM in the current directory or as specified by a COMSPEC environment variable. To return to QuickBASIC, enter the DOS command **EXIT**

### *Exit*

Leaves QuickBASIC and returns to DOS. If current
program has not been saved, you are asked whether you
want to save program before you exit.

# Edit Menu

The Edit menu's commands include the following:

### *Undo (Alt-Backspace)*

Restores to its original state the line currently being
edited. This command works only as long as cursor
remains on the line.

### *Cut (Shift-Del)*

Removes the text you have selected and places it in
Clipboard. Select text by holding down Shift key and
using cursor-movement keys to highlight text.

### *Copy (Ctrl-Ins)*

Places copy of the text you have selected into Clipboard without deleting it. Select text by holding down
Shift key and using cursor-movement keys to highlight
text.

### *Paste (Shift-Ins)*

Inserts copy of Clipboard's text into the file at cursor's
position. Use Cut or Copy commands before using this
command.

### *Clear (Del)*

Deletes selected text. Select text by holding down Shift
key and using cursor-movement keys to highlight text.

### *New SUB*

Creates a new SUB procedure and opens a window for
the entry and editing of the procedure. You also can type
SUB followed by the procedure's name and then press
Enter to create the procedure.

### New FUNCTION

Creates a new FUNCTION procedure and opens a window for you to enter and edit the procedure. You also can type FUNCTION followed by the procedure's name and then press Enter to create the procedure.

### Syntax Checking

Toggles off and on the syntax checking. A check mark next to this command specifies that syntax checking is enabled. Does not affect editing document files, for which syntax checking is always off.

# View Menu

The View menu's commands include the following:

### SUBs (F2)

Displays list of the modules and procedures in memory and allows selection of module or procedure to be displayed in View window.

### Next SUB (Shift-F2)

Alphabetically cycles through the procedures in a module, displaying the next one in the active window.

### Split

Splits View window horizontally or, if already split, clears bottom window. The F6 and Shift-F6 keys move between windows.

### Next Statement

Moves cursor to statement at which a suspended program will resume execution with the Continue command.

### Output Screen (F4)

Displays the screen on which program output is displayed.

### Include File

Allows viewing or editing of an include file. To use the command, place cursor on program line with the $INCLUDE metacommand and select **Include File** command.

### Included Lines

Specifies whether **Include File** command is to be used for viewing or for editing include files. Selecting this command toggles the option; check mark indicates include files are to be viewed only.

### Options

Specifies the display attributes (colors and highlighting) and several additional display options.

# Search Menu

The Search menu's commands include the following:

### Find

Searches forward from cursor position for next occurrence of specified text. Options are available for specifying search areas and restrictions.

### Selected Text (Ctrl-\)

Searches forward from cursor position for next occurrence of the text you have selected. Select text by holding down Shift key and using cursor-movement keys to highlight text.

### Repeat Last Find (F3)

Searches forward from cursor position for the text specified in the last use of **Find** command.

### Change (Ctrl-QA)

Searches for occurrence of the specified text and replaces that text with other text.

### Label

Searches forward from cursor position for next occurrence of a line label using currently selected text or text last specified in **Find** command. If no colon follows the text specified, one is appended automatically.

# Run Menu

The Run menu's commands include the following:

### Start (Shift-F5)

Executes program currently in memory.

### Restart

Resets all variables and places cursor on first executable statement.

### Continue (F5)

Continues program execution from statement where it was suspended or starts program from beginning if program is not running.

### Modify COMMAND$

Allows entry of a string that will be returned by the COMMAND$ function when the program is executed.

### Make EXE File

Compiles, links, and saves current program as an executable file. You specify whether program is to be compiled to a stand-alone .EXE file or one that requires the BRUN40.EXE run-time module.

### Make Library

Creates Quick Library consisting of currently loaded modules, along with modules included in any Quick Library loaded when QuickBASIC was started.

### Set Main Module

For programs with multiple modules, changes the module designated as the "main module," in which execution begins when the program is run.

# Debug Menu

The Debug menu's commands include the following:

### Add Watch

Allows entry of a watch expression, which causes the expression's value to be displayed in Watch window.

### Watchpoint

Allows entry of a relational expression as a watchpoint. Program execution is suspended when a watchpoint expression becomes *true* and may be resumed by using Continue command.

### Delete Watch

Removes highlighted watchpoint or watch expression from Watch window.

### Delete All Watch

Removes all watchpoints and watch expressions.

### Trace On

Toggles trace function on or off. Check mark next to command specifies that function is on.

### History On

Toggles on or off the recording of last 20 lines executed. Check mark next to command specifies that function is on.

### Toggle Breakpoint (F9)

Sets or clears a breakpoint at line on which cursor is located. Lines with breakpoints are highlighted. Program execution is suspended at each line at which a breakpoint has been set and may be resumed by using **Continue** command.

### Clear All Breakpoints

Removes all breakpoints.

### Set Next Statement

Continues execution of program at statement on which cursor is located. Has same effect as a GOTO statement.

# Calls Menu

This menu displays sequence of procedures called in getting to the procedure at which program execution has been suspended.

# Help Menu

The Help menu's commands include the following:

### General (F1)

Displays general information on editing and the shortcut keys, and an ASCII character table.

### Topic (Shift-F1)

Displays context-sensitive help information for keyword on which cursor is located or displays list of BASIC keywords for which information may be displayed.

### Close Help (Esc)

Terminates display of help information.

# Environment Keys and Mouse Operations

In QuickBASIC, many keyboard keys and key combinations have special functions. Use these keys (or a mouse) for editing text or other operations.

## Shortcut Keys

Most of the following keys are shortcuts for some menu commands. Other keys execute commands similar to but not available as menu commands.

| | |
|---|---|
| F1 | Help menu's **General** command |
| F2 | View menu's **SUBs** command |
| F3 | Search menu's **Repeat Last Find** command |
| F4 | View menu's **Output Screen** command |
| F5 | Run menu's **Continue** command |
| F6 | Shifts active window forward |
| F7 | Continues program execution to statement on which cursor is located |
| F8 | Executes the following program statement. This key is used for single-step execution. |
| F9 | Debug menu's **Toggle Breakpoint** command |
| F10 | Executes the following program statement or procedure. This key is used for single-step execution, stepping over procedures. |
| Shift-F1 | Help menu's **Topic** command |
| Shift-F2 | View menu's **Next SUB** command |
| Shift-F5 | Run menu's **Start** command |
| Shift-F6 | Shifts active window backward |

| Shift-F8 | Steps through history to previous statement executed |
| Shift-F10 | Steps through history to next statement executed |
| Ctrl-F2 | Cycles through procedures in a module in reverse alphabetical order. Opposite of Next SUB command on View menu. |
| Ctrl-F5 | Reduces full-screen window to its previous size |
| Ctrl-F10 | Expands active window to full screen or returns to split screen |
| Esc | Help menu's Close Help command |
| Del | Edit menu's Clear command |
| Shift-Ins | Edit menu's Paste command |
| Shift-Del | Edit menu's Cut command |
| Ctrl-Ins | Edit menu's Copy command |
| Ctrl-\ | Search menu's Find command |
| Ctrl-QA | Search menu's Change command |
| Alt-Backspace | Edit menu's Undo command |
| Alt-Plus | Expands active window |
| Alt-Minus | Contracts active window |
| Alt | Moves to menu bar to make menu selection |

# Editor Control Keys

The QuickBASIC editor allows use of either the special keys on the keyboard or the control-character key combinations used in WordStar®. For some operations, however, only one option is available. The following operations simply move the cursor or text; they do not alter the file.

| | |
|---|---|
| ↑<br>Ctrl-E | Moves cursor up one line |
| ↓<br>Ctrl-X | Moves cursor down one line |
| ←<br>Ctrl-S | Moves cursor left one character |
| →<br>Ctrl-D | Moves cursor right one character |
| Ctrl-←<br>Ctrl-A | Moves cursor left one word |
| Ctrl-→<br>Ctrl-F | Moves cursor right one word |
| Home<br>Ctrl-QS | Moves cursor to beginning of line |
| End<br>Ctrl-QD | Moves cursor to end of line |
| Ctrl-Enter<br>Ctrl-J | Moves cursor to beginning of next line |
| Ctrl-W | Scrolls text up one line |
| Ctrl-Z | Scrolls text down one line |
| Ctrl-QE | Moves cursor to top of window |
| Ctrl-QX | Moves cursor to bottom of window |
| PgUp<br>Ctrl-R | Scrolls text up one page |
| PgDn<br>Ctrl-C | Scrolls text down one page |
| Ctrl-PgUp | Scrolls text left one window |
| Ctrl-PgDn | Scrolls text right one window |
| Ctrl-Home<br>Ctrl-QR | Moves cursor to beginning of module or procedure |
| Ctrl-End<br>Ctrl-QC | Moves cursor to end of module or procedure |
| Ctrl-Q$n$<br>($n$=1 to 3) | Moves cursor to location of marker $n$ |

# Text-Selection Keys

You select text for block operations by holding down Shift key and using cursor-movement keys to move cursor and extend highlighted area. WordStar's control-key combinations do not work for selecting text.

| | |
|---|---|
| Shift-↑ | Selects line above |
| Shift-↓ | Selects current line |
| Shift-← | Selects character to left |
| Shift-→ | Selects character to right |
| Shift-Ctrl-← | Selects word to left |
| Shift-Ctrl-→ | Selects word to right |
| Shift-PgUp | Selects one screen up |
| Shift-PgDn | Selects one screen down |
| Shift-Ctrl-Home | Selects to beginning of module or procedure |
| Shift-Ctrl-End | Selects to end of module or procedure |

# Other Editing Keys

Some of the remaining editing functions use only the special keys on the keyboard; some use only the WordStar control-character combinations. A few use both.

| | |
|---|---|
| Enter | Inserts carriage return at cursor's location and leaves cursor on character following the return |
| Ctrl-N | Inserts carriage return at cursor's location and leaves cursor on character preceding the return |
| Ins<br>Ctrl-V | Toggles between insert and overtype modes |
| Ctrl-P Ctrl-*key* | Inserts control character associated with *key* |

| Ctrl-Kn (n=1 to 3) | Sets marker *n* at cursor's location |
| --- | --- |
| Del Ctrl-G | Deletes character at cursor or the selected text |
| Backspace Ctrl-H | Deletes character to left of cursor |
| Ctrl-T | Deletes a word |
| Ctrl-QY | Deletes from cursor to end of line. Saves deleted text in Clipboard. |
| Ctrl-Y | Deletes line. Saves deleted text in Clipboard. |
| Tab Ctrl-I | Moves cursor to next tab, inserting spaces |
| Shift-Tab | Deletes leading spaces for one tab position back |

# Mouse Operations

You can perform several QuickBASIC operations with a mouse. Use of a mouse with QuickBASIC is optional; all mouse operations described in this section can be performed also from keyboard.

| Select menu | Click on menu option |
| --- | --- |
| Select command | Click on command on menu |
| Select option | Click on option in dialog box |
| Select option | Double-click on option in dialog box and execute command |
| Scroll up one line in window | Click on ↑in vertical scroll bar |
| Scroll down one line in window | Click on ↓ in vertical scroll bar |
| Expand active window | Drag title bar up |
| Contract active window | Drag title bar down |

| Change active window | Click in window to be made active |
| Expand active window to full screen or return to split screen | Double-click on title or click on maximize icon |
| Execute program to selected line | Click right button on line |

# Creating Libraries and Programs

The program development process in QuickBASIC can involve the creation of libraries of program modules for use with multiple programs, the creation of executable programs that can be executed outside the QuickBASIC environment, and the debugging of programs.

## Creating and Using Libraries

A library is a collection of modules containing procedures that QuickBASIC programs use. You can generate libraries to make the same procedures available to all of the programs you develop. Libraries can include procedures written in QuickBASIC and in other programming languages.

QuickBASIC uses two types of libraries. A Quick Library (.QLB) is used when creating and running programs within the QuickBASIC environment. A stand-alone library (.LIB) is used when compiling QuickBASIC programs to .EXE files. Both forms must be available for complete program development.

To use a Quick Library, start QuickBASIC using the /l option to load the desired library. Add this option to the command line when you start QuickBASIC, as in

qb /l [*qlibname*]

where *qlibname* is the name of the Quick Library to be loaded. (The .QLB extension is optional.) If no *qlibname* is specified, QB.QLB (the Quick Library supplied with QuickBASIC) is loaded.

You can create a Quick Library by selecting the Make Library command from the Run menu. This creates both a Quick Library (.QLB) and a stand-alone library (.LIB) that includes all program modules currently loaded as well as the Quick Library modules loaded when QuickBASIC was started.

You may also create libraries from the DOS command line. This method is the only way to create libraries that include modules created with other languages. First, the program modules must be compiled or assembled into object (.OBJ) files. Then, the LINK program, to create a Quick Library by using this type of command:

> link /q *module*.obj [*module*.obj]...,*qlibname*.qlb,,
> bqlb40.lib;

The /q option specifies the creation of a Quick Library. The *module*.obj files are the names of the program module object files to be included in the library, and *qlibname*.qlb is the name for the Quick Library. Next you must use the LIB program to create a stand-alone library. You will use this library when you convert (compile) programs into .EXE files. The form of the command is

> lib *libname*.lib+*module*.obj [+*module*.obj]...

where *libname* is the same name that you gave to the Quick Library, and the program module object files are the same files that were included in the Quick Library.

# Creating Executable QuickBASIC Programs

You may convert (compile) QuickBASIC programs into .EXE files that may be executed from DOS either with or without the use of the QuickBASIC environ-

ment. If you do not use the QuickBASIC environment,
you will also need to link your programs. The final step
is to debug your programs.

# Compiling Programs

To create an .EXE file from within the QuickBASIC
environment, select the Make EXE File command from
the Run menu. This step compiles, links, and saves the
resulting program as an executable file.

You specify whether the program is to be compiled as a
stand-alone .EXE file or as a file that requires use of the
BRUN40.EXE run-time module. In the latter case, the
file BRUN40.EXE must be present on disk when
program is executed.

The Debug Code option in the dialog box specifies that
run-time checks for a number of error conditions are to
be included in the .EXE file.

To create an .EXE file for a BASIC program from
DOS, you must first compile all program modules into
object files and then link those object files into an
.EXE file. You compile BASIC program source files by
using the bc command in the following form:

> bc *sourcefile* [,[*objectfile*] [,[*listingfile*]]
> [*optionslist*];]

The *sourcefile* is the name of the BASIC program
module to be compiled. The two entries for *objectfile*
and *listingfile* optionally are used to specify the names to
be given to the object file being created and to the
source listing file. If you do not specify names for these
files, their names default to the same file name (without
the extension) as the source file, with the extensions
.OBJ and .LST, respectively. The *optionslist* includes
the command options listed in the following section.

You may also use the BASIC compiler by simply
entering bc on the DOS command line. In this case, the
compiler prompts for the required file names.

## Options for BC.EXE

When you are compiling a BASIC program module from DOS, you may enter the following options after the **bc** command:

| | |
|---|---|
| /a | Produces an assembly language listing of the object code |
| /ah | Allows individual dynamic arrays to exceed 64K |
| /c:*buffersize* | Sets the buffer size for the communications port |
| /d | Generates debugging code for run-time error checking. This option also enables Ctrl-Break. |
| /e | Indicates the presence of ON ERROR with RESUME statements |
| /mbf | Forces conversion functions to treat numbers as Microsoft Binary Format numbers |
| /o | Creates a stand-alone .EXE program that does not require the run-time module |
| /r | Stores arrays in row-major order for use with routines written in other languages |
| /s | Writes quoted strings to object file instead of to symbol table |
| /v | Enables event trapping, checking between statements for an event |
| /w | Enables event trapping, checking between lines for event |
| /x | Indicates the presence of ON ERROR with RESUME or RESUME NEXT |
| /zd | Produces an object file for use with the Microsoft Symbolic Debugger |
| /zi | Produces an object file for use with the Microsoft CodeView debugger |

# Linking Programs

After you have compiled all of the program modules
into object files, they must be linked to each other and to
the necessary libraries by using LINK.EXE. You may
specify the link operation's parameters on the command
line, in response to prompts, or in a response file. The
syntax for the command line is

> **link** *objfile* [,[*exefile*][,[*mapfile*]
> [,[*lib*]]] [*linkopts*][;]]

*Objfile* includes the names of one or more program
object files to be linked, separated by plus signs or
spaces. *Exefile* is the name that you specify for the
executable file. If you do not specify a file name, this
file receives the same root file name as the first object
file. If you want a listing file containing a symbol map
listing, specify the file name for *mapfile*. The *lib*
includes the names of the libraries named in the object
files (BRUN40.LIB is the default). You must specify
BCOM40.LIB if you specified it when compiling the
program modules; you must specify also any other
libraries used by the program. Further explanation of
LINK is beyond the scope of this quick reference. For
more information, see the Microsoft manuals or *Using
Assembly Language*, published by Que Corporation.

# Debugging Programs

To debug a program that is not operating correctly, you
execute the program until it is at or near the section that
you suspect is causing the problem. You then examine
the status of the program. If necessary, you can modify
the values of variables or statements. Then you resume
execution of the program until it reaches the next
questionable part.

### Executing Program Statements

You execute the current program in the normal manner
from its beginning by using Shift-F5 or the Run menu's

Start command. Execution continues until the program terminates normally, the program encounters an error, the operator presses Ctrl-Break, or until a debugging breakpoint or watchpoint suspends execution.

When program execution has been suspended, use F5 or the Run menu's Continue command to continue execution from the current statement. Pressing F7 causes a program to start (or resume) execution and to stop at the cursor's current position. The View menu's Set Next command selects a different statement as the starting point for resuming execution. To execute programs in slow motion, with the currently executing statement highlighted, select the Trace On command from the Debug menu.

Use the F8 key to "single-step" through the program. The F10 key performs the same function, except that it skips over procedures, executing them in a single step.

### Stopping Program Execution

A crude method of stopping program execution is to press Ctrl-Break. This key combination can also be used when you think the program is trapped in an infinite loop.

You can set breakpoints to stop program execution at specified statements. Place the cursor on the statement where you want the program to stop and select the Toggle Breakpoint command from the Debug menu. The statement is highlighted, and program execution is suspended when it reaches the statement.

You can use watchpoints to stop execution when the values of program variables (or expressions containing such variables) meet specified conditions. Select the Watchpoint command from the Debug menu and enter an expression in the Watch window. When the value of a watchpoint expression becomes *true*, program execution will be suspended.

The Calls menu displays the sequence of calls from one procedure to another with the current procedure displayed at the top of the list. By selecting another procedure, you can specify that the program suspend execution when it returns to that procedure.

### Examining and Modifying Suspended Programs

When program execution has been suspended, you can examine the status of the program and make modifications. To determine the value of any variable, move to the Immediate window and use a PRINT statement. Alternatively, use the Add Watch command to enter watch expressions into the Watch window. The value of the watch expressions is displayed continuously.

If you are executing the program with Trace On, or if you have enabled the History On command, you can examine the last 20 statements that were executed before the program was stopped. Use Shift-F8 and Shift-F10 to move backward and forward through these 20 program statements.

While program execution is suspended, you can change values of program variables by entering an assignment statement in the Immediate window. Program statements also may be changed when program execution is suspended. Some changes, however, can make it impossible to resume program execution.

# TROFF

*Statement*

### Syntax

TROFF

### Purpose

Turns off tracing of program.

# TRON

*Statement*

### Syntax

TRON

### Purpose

Turns on program tracing. Each statement is high-lighted when it executes in the QuickBASIC environment. For programs compiled to .EXE files, TRON displays line numbers if the program was compiled with Debug option in the QuickBASIC environment or with /d option with the bc command.

# Programming Essentials

QuickBASIC programs are composed of lines and statements, which, in turn, are made up of constants and variables, often combined into expressions using operators. QuickBASIC program lines may include a line identifier and one or more BASIC statements.

## Character Set

QuickBASIC uses upper- and lowercase alphabetic characters, numeric digits, and the following special characters:

SPACE ! " # $ % & ' ( ) * + ,

- . / : ; < = > ? @ [ \ ] ^ _

Use these characters for BASIC keywords and to create BASIC identifiers, such as variable and procedure names. To indicate the end of a line, press Enter for a carriage return (ASCII 13). All other characters available on the IBM® PC can be used within strings, discussed later in this section.

## Program Lines

Program lines may include up to 256 characters if entered within the QuickBASIC environment. When you use another editor to enter a program, use an underscore

( _ ) to indicate the continuation of one physical line to the next. Lines longer than 256 characters are then allowed.

The syntax of a BASIC program line is as follows:

> [*lineidentifier*]    [*statement*]
>             [ : *statement*] . . . [*comment*]

All of the elements are optional. Therefore, a program can contain blank lines. The *lineidentifier* may be either a *line number* or a *line label*. Line numbers, which must be in the range from 0 through 65,529, simply identify a line; they do not determine the order in which lines are executed.

Line labels are combinations of from 1 to 40 letters and digits. A line label must start with a letter and must be followed by a colon. The case of the letters is ignored.

BASIC program *statements* generally consist of a statement keyword, often followed by additional information. One exception is the assignment statement, for which the LET keyword is optional.

You may place multiple statements on a single program line, separated by colons (:), but this generally is not good programming practice and serves no useful purpose with QuickBASIC.

# REM

*Statement*

### Syntax

    REM *remark*
    ' *remark*

### Purpose

Allows explanatory remarks to be added to a program without affecting execution. Must be final statement on a program line. REM must be preceded by a colon on a multiple-statement line; the apostrophe form is not preceded by a colon. Both forms used also for entering metacommands.

# Program Structure

QuickBASIC programs can consist of one or more modules. Each module is a source file that you can compile separately. The main module contains the statements that are first executed when the program starts running. Execution is passed to other modules through SUB and FUNCTION procedure calls.

Modules include the statements in the module, called the *module-level code*, and may also contain SUB and FUNCTION procedures. Module-level code in modules other than the main module is used primarily for declarations and error-handling.

# Data Types, Constants, and Variables

The elementary data types may be used for constants and variables, including arrays and user-defined types.

## Elementary Data Types

QuickBASIC has six elementary data types that you can use within programs:

### Integer

Two-byte whole numbers ranging from –32,768 to 32,767

### Long Integer

Four-byte whole numbers ranging from –2,147,483,648 to 2,147,483,647

### Single-Precision

Four-byte floating point numbers accurate to about seven decimal places with magnitudes ranging from

$10^{-45}$ to $10^{38}$. (Accuracy is approximate because the values are stored as binary numbers.)

### Double-Precision

Eight-byte floating point numbers accurate to about 15 or 16 decimal places with magnitudes ranging from $10^{-324}$ to $10^{308}$. (Accuracy is approximate because the values are stored as binary numbers.)

### Fixed-Length String

Declared-length sequences of up to 32,767 characters

### Variable-Length String

Variable-length sequences of up to 32,767 characters

# Constants

Constants are values that do not change during program execution. QuickBASIC uses literal and symbolic constants. Symbolic constants are defined with the CONST statement and are similar to variables except that their values do not change.

Literal constants are the actual representations of the values and are of the following types:

### Integer

Values in the range of the integer type; hexadecimal values with prefix &H or &h; octal values with prefix &, &o, or &O

### Long Integer

Values in the range of the long integer type, including decimal, hexadecimal, and octal values as described for the integer type

### Fixed Point

Decimal numbers containing decimal points. The number may be as long as desired but (when used) only the significant digits that fit within a double-precision value are retained.

### Single-Precision Floating Point

Values in the range of the single-precision type expressed in exponential notation

### Double-Precision Floating Point

Values in the range of the double-precision type expressed in exponential notation

### String

Sequences of characters enclosed in quotation marks

# CONST

*Statement*

### Syntax

```
CONST constname = expr [, constname = expr] . . .
```

### Purpose

Defines symbolic constants by assigning value of *expression* to symbolic constant designated by *constant name*. Use symbolic constants like variables in expressions. Symbolic constants must be defined before they are used. String concatenation is not allowed for string expressions. Names of symbolic constants follow the rules for names of variables. Their types are defined either by use of a type-declaration character suffix (as for variables) or by the type of the expression.

# Variables

Variables are the names of objects to which values may be assigned. Variable names must begin with a letter and may consist of up to 40 characters, including letters, numbers, and the decimal point. Variable types include the elementary data types listed previously.

The variable type may be specified by appending a type-declaration suffix character to the end of the variable name. The type-declaration suffixes are

| % | Integer |
| & | Long integer |
| ! | Single-precision |
| # | Double-precision |
| $ | String |

The default type for variables without a type-declaration suffix is single-precision.

You can also specify variable type by using DEFINT, DEFLNG, DEFSNG, DEFDBL, and DEFSTR statements (see description for these keywords). Type-declaration suffixes take precedence over these declarations.

You can also specify the variable type in declaration statements using DIM, COMMON, REDIM, SHARED, or STATIC (see description for these keywords).

# DEFDBL

*Statement*

### Syntax

    DEFDBL letterrange [, letterrange]...

### Purpose

Defines as double-precision all variables with names beginning with letters in *letterrange*. The *letterrange* can be a single letter, such as K, or a range of letters, such as H–N.

# DEFINT

*Statement*

### Syntax

    DEFINT letterrange [, letterrange]...

### Purpose

Defines as integer all variables with names beginning
with letters in *letterrange*. The *letterrange* can be a
single letter, such as K, or a range of letters, such as
H–N.

# DEFLNG

*Statement*

### Syntax

```
DEFLNG letterrange [,letterrange]...
```

### Purpose

Defines as long integer all variables with names beginning with letters in *letterrange*. The *letterrange* can be a
single letter, such as K, or a range of letters, such as
H–N.

# DEFSNG

*Statement*

### Syntax

```
DEFSNG letterrange [,letterrange]...
```

### Purpose

Defines as single-precision all variables with names
beginning with letters in *letterrange*. The *letterrange*
can be a single letter, such as K, or a range of letters,
such as H–N.

# DEFSTR

*Statement*

### Syntax

```
DEFSTR letterrange [,letterrange]...
```

### Purpose

Defines as variable-length string all variables with names beginning with letters in *letterrange*. The *letterrange* can be a single letter, such as K, or a range of letters, such as H–N.

# Array Variables

An array is a collection of objects to which values may be assigned. An array has a single name; its elements are referenced by one or more numeric subscripts.

The number of array dimensions and the subscript ranges can be specified using the DIM statement. You specify the upper and lower bounds for these subscripts.

If the lower bound for a subscript is not specified, the value defaults to zero (or one if specified using the OPTION BASE statement). If an array is not explicitly dimensioned, the upper bound defaults to 10.

# DIM

*Statement*

### Syntax

```
DIM [SHARED] var[ (subs[ , subs] ... ) ]
    [AS type]  [ , var[ (subs[ , subs] ... ) ]
    [AS type]] ...
```

where *subs* = [*lower* TO ] *upper*

### Purpose

DIM statement's primary function is to declare the size of an array with the name *variable* by specifying maximum subscript value *upper* for each dimension and (optionally) minimum subscript value *lower*.

The *variable* can be declared to be of a specific type by adding the AS *type* clause where *type* can be INTEGER, LONG, SINGLE, DOUBLE, STRING, or a user-defined type.

When SHARED is specified, all procedures in a module are allowed to access *variables* in the statement.

Arrays declared with variables as subscripts or in COMMON statements are $DYNAMIC (space is allocated when program is run). Arrays dimensioned implicitly or with constants as subscripts are $STATIC (space is allocated when program is compiled).

# ERASE
*Statement*

### Syntax

```
ERASE array [,array]...
```

### Purpose

For $STATIC arrays, sets all elements of a numeric *array* to zero and sets all elements of a string *array* to null. For $DYNAMIC arrays, this statement deallocates the space occupied by the *array* and frees the memory.

# LBOUND
*Function*

### Syntax

```
LBOUND (array [,dimension])
```

### Purpose

Determines lowest subscript value for specified *dimension* of *array*. *Dimension* is the number of the dimension (1, 2, 3,...) and may be omitted for one-dimensional arrays. See also the UBOUND function.

# OPTION BASE
*Statement*

### Syntax

```
OPTION BASE n
```

### *Purpose*

Sets default for lowest subscript value for arrays. The value of *n* must be 0 or 1 (zero is the default). You must execute this statement before you dimension arrays. See DIM statement.

# REDIM

*Statement*

### *Syntax*

```
REDIM [SHARED] var [ (subs [ , subs ] ... ) ]
    [AS type] [ , var [ (subs [ , subs ] ... ) ]
    [AS type]] ...
```

where *subs* = [*lower* TO ] *upper*

### *Purpose*

Changes allocation of space to $DYNAMIC arrays. You cannot use this statement to change the number of dimensions of an array. This statement has same syntax and options as DIM statement.

# UBOUND

*Function*

### *Syntax*

UBOUND (*array* [ , *dimension*])

### *Purpose*

Determines highest subscript value for specified *dimension* of *array*. *Dimension* is the number of the dimension (1, 2, 3,...) and may be omitted for one-dimensional arrays. See also LBOUND function.

# User-Defined Data Types

QuickBASIC supports user-defined data types. These combine elementary data types (except variable-length strings) into a collection or record. Use the TYPE statement to define a new data type. The following example defines a type given the name Course, consisting of the elements Number, Title, and Code:

```
TYPE Course
    Number AS Integer
    Title  AS STRING*50
    Code   AS Integer
END TYPE
```

These types are used by declaring record variables to be of a given user-defined type. These declarations must be made using the DIM, COMMON, REDIM, SHARED, or STATIC statements as follows:

```
DIM NewCourse AS Course
```

The elements in a record variable are referred to with the name of the record variable followed by a period and the name of the element. For example, the following statement assigns the course number 233 to NewCourse:

```
NewCourse.Number = 233
```

User-defined types and record variables are especially helpful for random-access file input and output.

# TYPE END TYPE

*Statement*

## Syntax

```
TYPE typename
    elementname1 AS type1
    elementname2 AS type2
    .
    .
END TYPE
```

## Purpose

Specifies *type name* to be a user-defined variable type with *element name 1* being a variable of *type 1*, *element name 2* being a variable of *type 2*, and so forth. *Type name* and the *element names* follow rules for BASIC variable names. The *types* must be INTEGER, LONG, SINGLE, DOUBLE, or STRING*n* (fixed-length string).

# Operators, Expressions, and Assignment

You can combine variables with operators to create more complex expressions that can be used within other BASIC statements. The values of these expressions may also be assigned to other variables.

## Operators

Operators either precede a constant, variable, or expression or combine them to produce a new value. BASIC has arithmetic, relational, logical, string, and functional operators.

### Arithmetic Operators

You may use the following operators with numeric constants, variables, and expressions to perform arithmetic computations:

| | |
|---|---|
| + | Addition |
| − | Subtraction or negation |
| * | Multiplication |
| / | Division |
| ^ | Exponentiation |
| \ | Integer division (operands rounded to integers, quotient truncated to an integer) |
| MOD | Modulo arithmetic (the remainder resulting from an integer division) |

### Relational Operators

The following operators, used to compare two values in an expression, produce a result of true (−1) or false (0):

| = | Equal to |
| <> | Not equal to |
| < | Less than |
| > | Greater than |
| <= | Less than or equal to |
| >= | Greater than or equal to |

## *Logical Operators*

The following operators perform logical operations on expressions with values of true or false, producing a value of true or false:

NOT Logical not: NOT A reverses truth value of A

AND Logical and: A AND B is true if A is true and B is true

OR Logical or: A OR B is true if either A is true or B is true

XOR Exclusive or: A XOR B is true if A is true or if B is true but not if both are true

EQV Equivalence: A EQV B is true if both A and B are true or if both A and B are false

IMP Implication: A IMP B is true unless A is true and B is false

## *String Operator*

BASIC has a single string operator, which is used for combining two strings into a single string:

+ Concatenation

## *Functional Operators*

A functional operator performs an operation on an argument value and returns another value. A function has a name; the argument or arguments of the function are enclosed in parentheses following the name. Functions may be used in expressions just like constants, variables, and other expressions resulting from the use of the other operators.

QuickBASIC includes a large number of intrinsic (built-in) functions. You can define additional functions, which can be used in expressions just like the intrinsic functions.

# Order of Operations

When an expression includes multiple operators, the operations are performed in the following order:

| | |
|---|---|
| ^ | Exponentiation |
| – | Negation |
| * / | Multiplication, Division |
| \ | Integer Division |
| MOD | Modulo Arithmetic |
| + – | Addition, Subtraction |
| = <> < > <= >= | Relational Operations |
| NOT | Logical Not |
| AND | Logical And |
| OR | Logical Or |
| XOR | Exclusive Or |
| EQV | Equivalence |
| IMP | Implication |

Operations at the same level are performed from left to right. Operations inside parentheses are always performed first. You may nest parentheses.

# Expressions

You combine constants and variables with operators to produce expressions. Expressions are evaluated to produce values. You may include expressions within more complex expressions; you may assign the values of expressions to variables; and you may include expressions in most statements that require values.

### Numeric Expressions

You form numeric expressions by using numeric constants and variables, arithmetic operators, and function operators that return numeric values. The order of evaluation within a numeric expression is determined by the ordering of the operators listed previously and by parentheses.

You may mix constants and variables of different numeric data types within an expression. During the evaluation of expressions with mixed numeric types, the values are converted to the precision of the most precise operand and the results are returned to that degree of precision.

### String Expressions

You form string expressions by using string constants and variables, the string operator, and function operators that return string values. You may print string expressions. String expressions may be used as the arguments to functions of strings, in other string or logical expressions, or in BASIC statements requiring string values.

### Logical (Boolean) Expressions

The relational and logical operators are used to construct logical (boolean) expressions, which are evaluated to values of either true (–1) or false (0). You may include numeric expressions, string expressions, and other logical expressions within logical expressions.

Logical expressions are used most often within statements to control program flow. However, their numeric values may also be assigned to other variables and may be used within numeric expressions.

# Assignment

By using assignment statements, you may assign the values of constants, variables, and expressions to variables. Only numeric values may be assigned to numeric variables. If necessary, BASIC converts the value's numeric data type to the type required by the variable to which it is to be assigned. Only string values may be assigned to string variables.

**Statement**

### Syntax

    [LET] var = expr

### Purpose

Assigns the value of *expression* to the *variable*. The statement can assign the values of one record variable to another record variable if both record variables are of the same user-defined type.

**Statement**

### Syntax

    SWAP var1, var2

### Purpose

Assigns the value of *variable 1* to *variable 2* and assigns the value of *variable 2* to *variable 1*. The two variables must be of the same data type.

## Control of Program Flow

BASIC statements normally are executed sequentially in a program. You may use a number of BASIC statements to control program flow to allow repetition of groups of statements, selection of the statements to be executed based upon the values of logical expressions, and so forth. QuickBASIC includes several statements that allow the writing of structured programs, including the DO...LOOP structure, the multiline IF...THEN...ELSE structure, and the SELECT CASE structure.

# DO...LOOP

*Statements*

## Syntax

First version:
```
DO
    [statements]
LOOP [{WHILE | UNTIL} condition]
```

Second version:
```
DO [{WHILE | UNTIL} condition]
    [statements]
LOOP
```

## Purpose

Repeatedly executes *statements* either WHILE value of *condition* is true or UNTIL that value becomes true. The *condition* is evaluated each time it is encountered.

With *condition* at the end of the loop, the statements will always execute at least once. With *condition* at the loop's beginning, the statements will not be executed at all if the continuation condition is not met. With both forms, execution proceeds with the statement following the LOOP statement when the looping is completed.

# END

*Statement*

## Syntax

```
END
```

## Purpose

Causes normal termination of program execution. All files are closed. This statement is assumed at the end of a program and is not required.

# EXIT DO

*Statement*

### Syntax

```
EXIT DO
```

### Purpose

Terminates a `DO...LOOP` structure by transferring control to the statement following the `LOOP` statement.

# EXIT FOR

*Statement*

### Syntax

```
EXIT FOR
```

### Purpose

Terminates a `FOR...NEXT` loop by transferring control to the statement following the `NEXT` statement.

# FOR...NEXT

*Statement*

### Syntax

```
FOR indexvar = start TO end [STEP incr]
    [statements]
NEXT [indexvar [,indexvar]...]
```

### Purpose

Executes block of *statements*, increasing the value of *index variable* each time by the value of the *increment* until the value of *index variable* is greater than that of *end*. `STEP`, if not specified, is assumed to be one. If the value of *increment* is negative, the value of *index variable* is decreased until the value is less than the value of *end*. If the *start* value is greater than the *end* value, the *statements* are never executed. With nested `FOR...NEXT` loops, a `NEXT` without an *index variable* is matched with the most recent `FOR` statement.

# GOSUB

*Statement*

## Syntax

    GOSUB *lineident*

## Purpose

Transfers program execution to a subroutine beginning
with *line identifier*. Control is returned to statement
following the GOSUB by use of RETURN (see RETURN).
Subroutines may be used recursively.

# GOTO

*Statement*

## Syntax

    GOTO *lineident*

## Purpose

Transfers program execution to the statement specified
by the *line identifier*.

# IF...THEN...ELSE

*Statement*

## Syntax

Single-line:

    IF *condition* THEN {*ifstatements* | *linenum*}
        [ELSE {*elsestatements* | *linenum*}]

Block:

    IF *condition* THEN
        [*statements*]
    [ELSEIF *condition* THEN
        [*statements*]]

        .
        .

    [ELSE
        [*statements*]]
    END IF

### Purpose

You must write the single-line IF...THEN...ELSE statement on a single BASIC program line. If value of *condition* is true, the *if statements* are executed. Otherwise, the *else statements*, if any, are executed. The program continues execution on the next line. You must separate multiple *if* or *else statements* by colons. These statements may be replaced by a *line number* (not a label), in which case control is transferred to that line as if a GOTO statement had been entered. To transfer control to a line identified with a label, use the full statement GOTO *label*.

You have more flexible, structured programming with the block IF...THEN...ELSE statements. If value of first *condition* is true, the first group of *statements* is executed. This condition can be followed by further tests using ELSEIF statements. If any of those *conditions* is true, then the following group of *statements* is executed. With an ELSE statement, if none of the preceding *conditions* is true, the following *statements* would be executed. After the appropriate statements have been executed, execution continues with the statement following the END IF.

# ON...GOSUB

*Statement*

### Syntax

ON *expr* GOSUB *lineident* [ , *lineident*] . . .

### Purpose

Evaluates *expression* and then executes a GOSUB to the line with the *line identifier* in the list specified by the value of the expression. The RETURN statement in the subroutine transfers control back to the statement following the ON...GOSUB statement. For example, if *expression* has a value of two, the statement executes a GOSUB to the second *line identifier*. If the value of *expression* is zero or is greater than the number of *line identifiers* listed, then no branching occurs.

ON...GOSUB produces an error if *expression* is
negative or is greater than 255. The SELECT CASE
statement is a more effective method for selecting from
multiple options.

# ON...GOTO

*Statement*

### Syntax

ON *expr* GOTO *lineident* [ , *lineident*] . . .

### Purpose

Works exactly like the ON . . . GOSUB statement except
that it executes a GOTO (rather than a GOSUB) to line
with *line identifier*.

# RETURN

*Statement*

### Syntax

RETURN [ *lineident*]

### Purpose

Exits subroutine called with GOSUB, transferring
execution to statement following the GOSUB or to
statement specified by *line identifier*.

# SELECT CASE

*Statement*

### Syntax

```
SELECT CASE testexpr
CASE expressionlist1
    [statements1]
CASE expressionlist2
    [statements2]
        .
        .
    [CASE ELSE
```

```
        [statements n]]
    END SELECT
```

where *expression list* can include one or more entries of
the following form, separated by commas:

*expression*
*expression* TO *expression*
IS *relational-operator expression*

### Purpose

Executes one of a number of groups of statements based
on value of *test expression*, which is compared with the
entries in *expression lists*. If *test expression* matches an
entry in an *expression list*, the following group of
statements is executed and execution continues following the END SELECT statement. If no match is found,
any *statements* following CASE ELSE are executed. If
CASE ELSE is omitted and no match is found, an error
is generated.

# STOP

*Statement*

### Syntax

```
    STOP
```

### Purpose

Suspends program execution. Within QuickBASIC
environment, STOP leaves files open; you can continue
program by selecting the **Continue** command. In a
stand-alone .EXE program, STOP closes files.

# WHILE...WEND

*Statements*

### Syntax

```
    WHILE condition
        [statements]
    WEND
```

*Purpose*

Repeatedly executes block of *statements* while value of *condition* is true. `DO...LOOP` is a more general and powerful form of the `WHILE...WEND` statements.

# Functions and Subprograms

`SUB` and `FUNCTION` procedures provide powerful means for dividing programs into sections that perform different activities. The `DEF FN` functions return individual values similar to `FUNCTION` procedures.

## *Procedures*

The two types of procedures are `FUNCTION` and `SUB`. Within the QuickBASIC environment, you create these procedures by using the **New FUNCTION** and **New SUB** commands. This method results in keeping the procedure code separate from the module-level code. Procedure code is displayed in a separate window. Both types of procedures can be called recursively.

## FUNCTION Procedures

`FUNCTION` procedures return a single value and may be used within expressions. Besides returning a value, a `FUNCTION` can change the value of any variables passed as parameters.

Enter a `FUNCTION` by selecting the **New FUNCTION** command. You use a `FUNCTION` by including its name within an expression, followed (in parentheses) by any parameters. The following example calculates compound interest:

```
FUNCTION CompoundInt (Principal,
    IntRate, Periods)
  CompoundInt = Principal *
```

```
              (1 + IntRate) ^ Periods
     END FUNCTION
```

To use a FUNCTION in a module other than the one in which it is defined, you must enter the declaration of the FUNCTION in the module in which it is to be used. To use the sample FUNCTION in another module, you would use the following statement:

```
DECLARE FUNCTION CompoundInt(
        OldBalance,CurrentInterest,1)
```

# SUB Procedures

SUB procedures are called by a separate statement and do not return a value like the FUNCTION procedures. Variables are passed to a SUB procedure in a parameter list; the SUB procedure can change the values of these variables, as well as perform other actions.

Enter a SUB procedure by using the New SUB command from the Edit menu. The following is an example of a SUB procedure for calculating compound interest:

```
SUB CompoundInt(Amt, Principal,
       IntRate,Periods)
   Amt = Principal * (1 + IntRate)
       ^ Periods
END SUB
```

The SUB procedure then is used with a CALL statement to perform the computations performed by the sample FUNCTION procedure, as follows:

```
CALL CompoundInt(NewBal,OldBal,
        CurrentInt,1)
```

If you declare a SUB procedure, the procedure may be used without the CALL keyword. If the SUB procedure is defined in another module, you must declare a SUB procedure in the module in which it is to be used. The declaration for the sample SUB procedure is

```
DECLARE SUB CompoundInt(Amt,
        Principal,IntRate,Periods)
```

This declaration, if included in a module, can be invoked as follows:

```
CompundInt(NewBal, OldBal,
        CurrentInt, 1)
```

# Passing Parameters

Argument variables in FUNCTION and SUB procedures normally are passed to the procedure by reference. The procedure is given access to the names of the variables and may modify their values. Constants and expressions used as arguments are passed by value. The procedure is given the value but has no variable to modify. To pass individual variables to procedures by value, enclose the variables in parentheses.

# Procedure Variables

Variables used within FUNCTION and SUB procedures normally are initialized when the procedure is invoked. These variables, known as automatic variables, are the default. You can also make variables in procedures static, meaning that they retain their values from one invocation to the next. Adding the keyword STATIC to the FUNCTION or SUB statement makes all variables in the procedure static. Alternatively, you may include a STATIC statement within the procedure to make selected variables static.

### Scope of Variables

Variables and symbolic constants may either be global (they can be accessed from anywhere within a module) or local (they can be accessed only from within the module-level code or from within a procedure).

Variables are local unless specified otherwise. A variable within a module's module-level code can be accessed only from that module. A variable in a procedure can be accessed only from within that procedure.

Symbolic constants are global if declared in the module-level code but local if declared within a procedure.

You can make variables global and accessible throughout a module by declaring them to be SHARED within a DIM, REDIM, or COMMON statement. You may use global variables in module-level code as well as in all procedures.

You can share local variables between a procedure and the module-level code by using the SHARED statement in the procedure. This statement specifies that the variable is to be accessible both to the module-level code and within the procedure.

# CALL

*Statement*

### Syntax

    CALL subname [ (arg [,arg]...) ]
    subname  [arg [,arg]...]

### Purpose

Causes the SUB procedure *subname* to be executed. Any *arguments* passed to the SUB procedure are separated by commas. To pass arrays as arguments, use the array name followed by empty parentheses. The default is to call by reference for variable arguments, but you may call an argument by value by placing the name of the variable inside parentheses. If you have declared the SUB procedure using a DECLARE statement, you may omit the keyword CALL and use the second form.

# DECLARE FUNCTION

*Statement*

### Syntax

    DECLARE FUNCTION name [ (arg [AS type]
        [,arg [AS type]]...) ]

*Purpose*

> Declaration of FUNCTION procedure *name*. Required if
> FUNCTION is defined in another module. Specifies the
> number and, optionally, *types* of *arguments* for checking
> function calls. The *type* may be any variable type except
> for fixed-length strings. If you omit the parentheses and
> argument list, no checking is done.

# DECLARE SUB

*Statement*

*Syntax*

> DECLARE SUB *name* [ (*arg* [AS *type*]
>     [, *arg* [AS *type*]]...)]

*Purpose*

> Declaration of SUB procedure *name*. Required if
> procedure is to be called without the CALL keyword or
> is defined in another module. The statement works
> exactly like the DECLARE FUNCTION statement.

# EXIT FUNCTION

*Statement*

*Syntax*

> EXIT FUNCTION

*Purpose*

> Terminates a FUNCTION procedure.

# EXIT SUB

*Statement*

*Syntax*

> EXIT SUB

*Purpose*

> Terminates a SUB procedure.

# FUNCTION

*Statements*

### Syntax

```
FUNCTION name [ (arg [AS type] [, arg
    [AS type]]...)] [STATIC]
    [statements]
    name = expr
    [statements]
END FUNCTION
```

### Purpose

Defines the FUNCTION procedure *name*. Argument list is as specified in the DECLARE FUNCTION statement. STATIC specifies that the local variables are preserved between calls to the procedure.

# SHARED

*Statement*

### Syntax

```
SHARED var [AS type] [, var
    [AS type]]...
```

### Purpose

Used within a FUNCTION or SUB procedure to specify that the *variables* declared at the module level are to be accessible within the procedure. The *type* may be any variable type.

# STATIC

*Statement*

### Syntax

```
STATIC var[()] [AS type] [, var[()]
    [AS type]]...
```

### Purpose

Used within a FUNCTION or SUB procedure or a DEF FN function to specify that the *variables* are to be local

to the procedure and are to be preserved between calls to
the procedure. The *type* may be any variable type.

# SUB

*Statements*

### Syntax

```
SUB name [ (arg [AS type] [, arg
   [AS type]] ...)] [STATIC]
     [statements]
END SUB
```

### Purpose

Defines the SUB procedure *name*. Argument list is as
specified in the DECLARE FUNCTION statement.
STATIC specifies that the local variables are preserved
between calls to the procedure.

## DEF FN Functions

The DEF FN functions return single values and may be
used within expressions. The names must always begin
with the letters *FN*. DEF FN functions are part of the
module-level code and may not be used from another
module. Because arguments are passed by value,
variables may not be modified by the function. The
function definition must come before the first use of the
function. You may not use the functions recursively.

# DEF FN

*Statements*

### Syntax

Single-line function:
```
DEF FNname [ (arg [AS type] [, arg
   [AS type]] ...) = expr
```

Multiple-line function:
```
DEF FNname [ (arg [AS type] [, arg
   [AS type]] ...)]
```

```
         [statements]
         FNname = expr
         [statements]
     END DEF
```

## Purpose

Defines the function with the name FN*name*. Name must begin with *FN*. Argument list is as specified for the DECLARE FUNCTION statement. The function is called by value and returns a single value. Variables not in the list of arguments are global. Function has access to variables in module.

# EXIT DEF

*Statement*

## Syntax

```
    EXIT DEF
```

## Purpose

Terminates a multiple-line DEF FN function.

# Numeric and String Functions and Operations

QuickBASIC includes numeric and string functions that can be used within expressions and statements that can perform additional string operations.

## Numeric Functions

Numeric functions generate numeric values. These values are the functions of the numeric expressions' values that serve as function arguments. Included among QuickBASIC's numeric functions are mathematical and trigonometric functions, functions for converting numbers from one type to another, and the RND function and RANDOMIZE statement for random-number generation.

*Function*

---

*Syntax*

ABS(*numexpr*)

---

*Purpose*

Determines absolute value of *numeric expression*. Negative values are changed to positive; positive values are unchanged. ABS returns a value of the same type as *numeric expression*.

*Function*

---

*Syntax*

ATN (*numexpr*)

---

*Purpose*

Calculates arctangent of the value of *numeric expression*. ATN returns result in radians as a single-precision value unless *numeric expression* is double-precision.

*Function*

---

*Syntax*

CDBL (*numexpr*)

---

*Purpose*

Converts value of numeric expression to a double-precision value.

# CINT

*Function*

### Syntax

CINT (*numexpr*)

### Purpose

Converts value of *numeric expression* to an integer value by rounding. The *numeric expression* must be in the range of –32,768 to 32,767; otherwise, an error results.

# CLNG

*Function*

### Syntax

CLNG (*numexpr*)

### Purpose

Converts value of *numeric expression* to a long integer. Must be in the range of –2,147,483,648 to 2,147,483,647; otherwise, an error results.

# COS

*Function*

### Syntax

COS (*numexpr*)

### Purpose

Calculates cosine of value of *numeric expression,* which must be in radians. Returns a single-precision value unless *numeric expression* is double-precision.

# CSNG

*Function*

### Syntax

CSNG (*numexpr*)

### Purpose

Converts value of *numeric expression* to a single-precision value by rounding.

*Function*

### Syntax

EXP (*numexpr*)

### Purpose

Calculates the exponential function, the value of *e* (the base of the natural logarithms, 2.71828...) raised to the power of the value of *numeric expression*. Produces an error if the value of *numerical expression* is greater than 88.02969. EXP returns the result as a single-precision value unless *numeric expression* is double-precision. EXP is the inverse of the LOG function.

*Function*

### Syntax

FIX (*numexpr*)

### Purpose

Converts value of *numeric expression* to an integer value by truncation, dropping any digits following the decimal point. The *numeric expression* must be in the range of –32,768 to 32,767; otherwise, an error results.

*Function*

### Syntax

INT (*numexpr*)

### Purpose

Converts value of *numeric expression* to an integer by returning a value less than or equal to *numeric expression*. The *numeric expression* must be in the range of −32,768 to 32,767; otherwise, an error results.

# LOG

*Function*

### Syntax

LOG (*numexpr*)

### Purpose

Calculates the natural logarithm of *numeric expression*. Produces an error if *numeric expression* is less than or equal to zero. Returns a single-precision value unless *numeric expression* is double-precision.

# RANDOMIZE

*Statement*

### Syntax

RANDOMIZE [*numexpr*]

### Purpose

Reseeds random-number generator so that RND function returns a new sequence of random numbers. The *numeric expression* must be in the range −32,768 to 32,767. If no *numeric expression* is given, QuickBASIC prompts for one. Use the TIMER function for *numeric expression* to provide an arbitrary seed to produce different sequences of random numbers.

# RND

*Function*

### Syntax

RND[(*numexpr*) ]

### Purpose

Generates a single-precision random number in the range zero to one. With no *numeric expression* (or if the value of *numeric expression* is greater than zero) RND returns the next random number generated. If *numeric expression* is equal to zero, RND returns the last number generated. If *numeric expression* is less than zero, RND returns a number that is always the same for each value of *numeric expression*.

*Function*

### Syntax

SGN (*numexpr*)

### Purpose

Determines sign of the value of *numeric expression*. Returns 1 if *numeric expression* is greater than zero, 0 if it equals zero, and −1 if it is less than zero.

*Function*

### Syntax

SIN (*numexpr*)

### Purpose

Calculates sine of the value of *numeric expression*, which must be in radians. SIN returns the result as a single-precision value unless *numeric expression* is double-precision.

*Function*

### Syntax

SQR (*numexpr*)

### Purpose

Calculates square root of the value of *numeric expression*. SQR produces an error if *numeric expression* is less than zero. SQR returns the result as a single-precision value unless *numeric expression* is double-precision.

# TAN

*Function*

### Syntax

TAN (*numexpr*)

### Purpose

Calculates tangent of the value of *numeric expression*, which must be in radians. TAN returns the result as a single-precision value unless *numeric expression* is double-precision.

# String Statements and Functions

String functions can extract portions of strings; string statements can insert strings into other strings. Quick-BASIC also has functions for determining the length of strings and the positions of strings within strings, for converting strings from upper- to lowercase (and vice versa), and for converting strings to numeric values and ASCII character codes (and vice versa).

 # ASC

*Function*

### Syntax

ASC (*strexpr*)

### Purpose

Returns the integer ASCII value of first character in *string expression*. ASC produces an error if *string expression* has a null value. This function is the inverse of the CHR$ function.

# CHR$

*Function*

### Syntax

CHR$ (*ASCIIcode*)

### Purpose

Generates a one-character string with designated *ASCII code*. The *ASCII code* must be in the range from 0 to 255. This function is the inverse of the ASC function.

# HEX$

*Function*

### Syntax

HEX$ (*numexpr*)

### Purpose

Produces string with hexadecimal representation of *numeric expression*. This function rounds *numeric expression* to an integer or long integer.

# INSTR

*Function*

### Syntax

INSTR ([*start*,] *strexpr1*, *strexpr2*)

### Purpose

Searches through *string expression 1* for first occurrence of *string expression 2* and returns numerical value of the beginning position. The *start* is an optional numerical value directing that the search begin at that character position in *string expression 1;* if you do not specify a value, search begins with first character. If no match is found, a value of zero is returned. If *string expression 2* is a null string, the function returns a value of 1 or value of *start*.

# LCASE$

*Function*

### Syntax

LCASE$ (*strexpr*)

### Purpose

Converts uppercase characters in *string expression* to lowercase. This function is the opposite of UCASE$.

# LEFT$

*Function*

### Syntax

LEFT$ (*strexpr, numexpr*)

### Purpose

Extracts from *string expression* the leftmost number of characters specified by *numeric expression*, which must have a value in the range of 0 to 32,767. If *numeric expression* is greater than length of *string expression*, LEFT$ returns entire *string expression*. See also MID$ and RIGHT$.

# LEN

*Function*

### Syntax

LEN (*strexpr*)

### Purpose

Determines number of characters in *string expression*. LEN returns an integer value.

# LSET

*Statement*

#### Syntax

    LSET *strvar* = *strexpr*

#### Purpose

Places *string expression* left-justified in *string variable*, filling any remaining spaces with blanks. If *string expression* is longer than length of *string variable*, statement truncates characters from end of *string expression*. For right-justification, use RSET.

# LTRIM$

*Function*

#### Syntax

    LTRIM$ (*strexpr*)

#### Purpose

Removes any leading spaces from left portion of *string expression*. To remove trailing spaces, use RTRIM$.

# MID$

*Function*

#### Syntax

    MID$ (*strexpr*, *start* [, *length*])

#### Purpose

Extracts from *string expression* the string with number of characters specified by *length*, beginning with character at position specified by *start*. If *start* is greater than the length of *string expression*, function returns a null string. If fewer characters than *length* are to the right of *start* or if *length* is not specified, function returns all characters in *string expression* from *start* to the end. See also LEFT$ and RIGHT$.

## MID$

***Statement***

### Syntax

    MID$ (strvar, start, [length]) = strexpr

### Purpose

Inserts *string expression* into *string variable* beginning
at character position specified by *start* and extending for
the number of characters specified by *length*. If you do
not specify *length*, as much of *string expression* is
inserted into the *string variable* as will fit in the existing
length of *string variable*. The MID$ statement inserts
one string into another, whereas the MID$ function
extracts one string from another.

## OCT$

***Function***

### Syntax

    OCT$ (numexpr)

### Purpose

Produces string with octal representation of *numeric
expression*. This function rounds *numeric expression* to
an integer or long integer.

## RIGHT$

***Function***

### Syntax

    RIGHT$ (strexpr, numexpr)

### Purpose

Extracts from *string expression* the rightmost number of
characters specified by *numeric expression*. The *numeric
expression* must be in the range from 0 to 32,767. If
*numeric expression* is greater than length of *string
expression*, returns entire *string expression*.

# RSET

*Statement*

### Syntax

RSET *strvar* = *strexpr*

### Purpose

Places *string expression* right-justified in *string variable*, filling any remaining spaces with blanks. If *string expression* is longer than current length of *string variable*, the statement truncates characters from end of *string expression*. For left-justification, use LSET.

# RTRIM$

*Function*

### Syntax

RTRIM$ (*strexpr*)

### Purpose

Removes any trailing spaces from right portion of *string expression*. To remove leading spaces, use LTRIM$.

# SPACE$

*Function*

### Syntax

SPACE$ (*numexpr*)

### Purpose

Produces string with length specified by *numeric expression*, filled with spaces. The *numeric expression* must be in the range 0 to 32,767.

# STR$

*Function*

### Syntax

STR$ (*numexpr*)

### Purpose

Produces string with numeric representation of value of *numeric expression*. String contains the characters that would be output by printing *numeric expression* with a BASIC PRINT statement, including a trailing blank and a leading blank if *numeric expression* is positive. This function is the inverse of the VAL function.

# STRING$

*Function*

### Syntax

```
STRING$ (numexpr, ASCIIcode)
STRING$ (numexpr, strexpr)
```

### Purpose

Produces a string with the length specified by *numeric expression*, filled with either the character specified by *ASCII code* or the first character in *string expression*. The *numeric expression* must be in the range 0 to 32,767. The *ASCII code* must be in the range 0 to 255.

# UCASE$

*Function*

### Syntax

```
UCASE$ (strexpr)
```

### Purpose

Converts to uppercase all lowercase characters in *string expression*. UCASE$ works in opposite direction from LCASE$.

# VAL

*Function*

### Syntax

```
VAL (strexpr)
```

#### Purpose

Determines numeric value represented by a string of digits in the *string expression*. VAL (the inverse of the STR$ function) interprets characters in *string expression* up to point of a character that cannot be interpreted as part of a number.

# Keyboard Input

Statements and functions are available to allow the user to enter information from the keyboard while the program is executing. Function keys may be assigned special expressions.

## *Character Input*

The INPUT statement is perhaps the simplest method of obtaining keyboard input. The user types values that are assigned to variables. Because INPUT has problems dealing with entries that contain commas or quotation marks, the user can easily make errors. LINE INPUT overcomes some of these problems by assigning an entire line of characters to a string variable. The INKEY$ function returns individual keypresses.

**INKEY$**

*Function*

#### Syntax

INKEY$

#### Purpose

Reads the keyboard, returning a string value with the result. Actual characters are returned as one-byte strings. Extended codes are returned as two-byte strings with first character being the null character (ASCII 0).

# INPUT$

*Function*

### Syntax

```
INPUT$(n)
```

### Purpose

Reads *n* characters from the keyboard. This function does not echo characters to the screen.

# INPUT

*Statement*

### Syntax

```
INPUT [;] ["promptstr"] {; | ,}] var
      [,var]...
```

### Purpose

Reads values entered on input line and assigns them to *variables* specified. Optional first semicolon indicates that cursor is not to be moved to next line after statement has been executed. Optional *prompt string* prints a message on input line. Semicolon following *prompt string* prints question mark after prompt, but a comma does not. The *variables* may be of any simple type. In responding to the INPUT statement, user must enter values for variables, separated by commas. If entries do not match *variable* type, an error occurs.

# LINE INPUT

*Statement*

### Syntax

```
LINE INPUT [;] ["promptstr";] strvar
```

### Purpose

Reads a line of characters and assigns them to *string variable*. Works similar to the INPUT statement.

# Function Keys

You use the KEY statement to assign "softkey" string values to the 10 (or 12) function keys. These values will then be entered whenever user presses a function key in response to requests for user input .

**KEY**

*Statement*

### Syntax

    KEY n, *strexpr*

### Purpose

Assigns *string expression* of up to 15 characters to function key *n*. When user presses function key, key enters characters in *string expression*. This statement uses *n* values of 30 and 31 for function keys F11 and F12. To disable a previously-assigned *string expression,* assign a null string to a key.

**KEY LIST**

*Statement*

### Syntax

    KEY LIST

### Purpose

Lists on-screen the full 15-character function key assignments for all function keys.

**KEY OFF**

*Statement*

### Syntax

    KEY OFF

*Purpose*

Turns off display of function key assignments on screen's bottom line.

# KEY ON

*Statement*

*Syntax*

```
KEY ON
```

*Purpose*

Displays across screen's bottom line the first six characters of each *string expression* assigned to a function key.

# Video Display Control

The SCREEN statement establishes video display mode. The COLOR statement specifies colors to be used. The PALETTE statements optionally specify which of a larger set of colors is to be assigned to the set of attributes to be used for the COLOR statement.

# CLS

*Statement*

*Syntax*

```
CLS [{0|1|2}]
```

*Purpose*

Erases screen and moves cursor to upper left corner. Without a number, active viewport is cleared. CLS 0 erases entire screen; CLS 1 erases graphics viewport; and CLS 2 erases text viewport.

# COLOR

*Statement*

## Syntax

Mode 0:
    COLOR  [*foreground*]  [, [*background*]
            [,*border*] ]

Mode 1:
    COLOR  [*background*]  [, *palette*]

Modes 7–10:
    COLOR  [*foreground*]  [, *background*]

Modes 11–13:
    COLOR  [*foreground*]

## Purpose

Specifies colors to be used on video display. Operation depends on SCREEN mode. See the SCREEN statement for video display modes and colors. Use the PALETTE statement in modes 7–13 and in setting background colors in modes 11–13.

# PALETTE

*Statement*

## Syntax

PALETTE  [*attrib*, *color*]

## Purpose

Associates *color* with the *attribute* for EGA, MCGA, and VGA display adapters. *Color* must be a long integer for modes 11–13. With no *attribute* or *color* specified, this statement resets colors to the defaults. See the SCREEN statement for colors.

# PALETTE USING

*Statement*

### Syntax

```
PALETTE USING array [ (index) ]
```

### Purpose

Associates the colors specified in *array* with the *index* values as attributes. The *index* specifies first element to be used. Number of elements starting with *index* must be sufficient to specify all colors for mode. The *array* must be a long integer for modes 11–13; integer for others.

# PCOPY

*Statement*

### Syntax

```
PCOPY source, destination
```

### Purpose

Copies *source* screen page to *destination* page. The page range is determined by adapter and mode.

# SCREEN

*Statement*

### Syntax

```
SCREEN [mode] [,[switch] [,[writepage]]
       [,[displpage]]]]
```

### Purpose

Specifies display mode, colors, and pages. When *switch* is specified and is zero, displays images in monochrome in mode 1 and the opposite in mode 0. The *write page* and *display page* are the numbers of the video pages to use. Number of pages depends on *mode* and display adapter. The display *modes* are as follows:

| Mode | Text Resltn | Graphics Resltn | Max Colors | Max Attributes | Adapters |
|---|---|---|---|---|---|
| 0 | Varying | None | 16 | 2 (16 EGA) | All |
| 1 | 40 × 25 | 320 × 200 | 16 | 4 | CGA,EGA, MCGA,VGA |
| 2 | 80 × 25 | 640 × 200 | 16 | 2 | CGA,EGA, MCGA,VGA |
| 9 | 80 × 25 80 × 43 | 640 × 350 | 64 | 16 | EGA,VGA |
| 10 | 80 × 25 80 × 43 | 640 × 350 | 9 Mono | 4 | EGA,VGA |
| 11 | 80 × 30 80 × 60 | 640 × 480 | 256K | 2 | MCGA,VGA |
| 12 | 80 × 30 80 × 60 | 640 × 480 | 256K | 16 | VGA |
| 13 | 40 × 25 | 320 × 200 | 256K | 256 | MCGA,VGA |

*Requires that you run QBHERC.COM before entering QuickBASIC or executing program.

# Text Output to Screen and Printer

This section describes the statements and functions related to printing text to the screen and printer. Printing to the screen is dependent on the settings for mode and color as described in the previous section.

## Controlling the Output Environment

QuickBASIC allows you to set the size of the text screen and the printer width, establish a text viewport, and determine the character and color at any cursor location.

## SCREEN

*Function*

### Syntax

```
SCREEN(row, col [,color])
```

### Purpose

Determines ASCII value of character at *row* and *column*.
If *color* is not zero, determines color's number.

# VIEW PRINT

*Statement*

### Syntax

```
VIEW PRINT [top TO bottom]
```

### Purpose

Sets viewport in which text printing can take place (*top*
is top line of viewport; *bottom* is bottom line).

# WIDTH

*Statement*

### Syntax

```
WIDTH [cols] [, lines]
WIDTH LPRINT width
```

### Purpose

Sets text screen width at 40 or 80 *columns* and optionally sets numbers of lines to any value allowed by
display adapter and screen mode.

## Locating the Cursor

With the following statement and functions, you can
determine the current cursor and print positions and
move cursor on the screen.

# CSRLIN

*Function*

### Syntax

```
CSRLIN
```

### Purpose

Returns an integer indicating line on which cursor is located.

# LOCATE

*Statement*

### Syntax

    LOCATE [line] [, [col] [, [display] [, [top]
           [,bottom]]]]

### Purpose

Positions cursor at *line* and *column* specified. This statement makes cursor invisible if *display* is zero, visible if *display* is one. *top* and *bottom* scan lines specified determine cursor's size.

# LPOS

*Function*

### Syntax

    LPOS(n)

### Purpose

Determines next print position for LPRINT statements. The *n* is the number of LPT*n*: port.

# POS

*Function*

### Syntax

    POS(numexpr)

### Purpose

Determines column in which cursor is located. This function returns an integer value. The *numeric expression* is not used.

# Character Output Statements

Use the following statements and functions to print text to the screen and the line printer.

## LPRINT

*Statement*

### Syntax

```
LPRINT [,] [expr [{,|;} [expr]]...]
```

### Purpose

Prints to line printer LPT1:. This statement works like the PRINT statement.

## LPRINT USING

*Statement*

### Syntax

```
LPRINT USING formatstr; [expr [; [expr]]...]
        [{,|;}]
```

### Purpose

Prints to line printer LPT1:. This statement works like the PRINT USING statement.

## PRINT

*Statement*

### Syntax

```
PRINT [,] [expr [{,|;} [expr]]...]
```

### Purpose

Prints values of *expressions* to the screen. Commas cause printing to begin at next 14-column print zone. Semicolons (or spaces) do not insert spaces before printing next expression. Without final punctuation, PRINT moves print position to next line. PRINT

statement with nothing following prints a blank line.
Text exceeding screen width automatically wraps to next
line.

PRINT statement prints numbers with leading space or
minus sign and trailing space. Floating-point numbers
are printed as fixed-point if value can be printed without
loss of accuracy in 7 columns for single-precision values
and 16 columns for double-precision values; otherwise,
they are printed as floating-point exponential numbers.

# PRINT USING

*Statement*

### Syntax

```
PRINT USING formatstr; [expr [; [expr]]...]
        [{,|;}]
```

### Purpose

Prints values of *expressions* as specified by *format
string*. If a numeric value is too large for the field
specified, prints % in front of the value. The following
character entries are valid for use in *format string*:

| | |
|---|---|
| # | Print one digit of a number. This specifies one position in number field. |
| . | Print decimal point. |
| , | Insert to left of decimal point to print commas between groups of thousands. This also specifies one position in number field. |
| + | Print sign of value (plus or minus) in position specified, at beginning or end of number. |
| – | Print minus sign at end of number (if negative). |
| $$ | Print dollar sign immediately preceding number. This also specifies two positions in number field. |
| ** | Print leading asterisks for number. This also specifies two positions in number field. |
| **$ | Print leading asterisks and dollar sign. This also specifies three positions in number field. |

^^^^ Print number in floating-point exponential
format, specifying exponential portion of
number. Use five carets for large exponents.

!    Print only first character in a string.

\ \  Print specified number of characters in a string,
where number is determined by number of
spaces plus backslashes.

&    Print entire string of whatever length.

_    Print following character in format string.

# SPC

*Function*

### Syntax

SPC(*n*)

### Purpose

Causes *n* spaces to be printed in PRINT or LPRINT
statement.

# TAB

*Function*

### Syntax

TAB(*col*)

### Purpose

Used in PRINT or LPRINT statement to move cursor or
print position to *column* specified. If current position is
past *column*, moves to next line. *Column* values greater
than the line width cause output to wrap to next line.
*Column* values less than one are equivalent to one.

# WRITE

*Statement*

### Syntax

WRITE [*expr* [, [*expr*]...]

### Purpose

Prints values of *expressions* to the screen, separated by
commas, with strings enclosed in quotation marks.
WRITE is used most often in WRITE# form for writing
to sequential files.

# File Input and Output

This section describes characteristics of files, explains
how to use them, and provides examples of the statements required to use the file types.

## *Sequential-Access Files*

A sequential file is a text file of ASCII characters.
Records are of variable length and delimited by the
carriage-return and line-feed characters (CR/LF).
Numeric or string values within records are delimited by
commas.

You must open sequential files in either INPUT,
OUTPUT, or APPEND mode. In OUTPUT mode, Quick-
BASIC writes information to the file from the beginning, whereas in APPEND mode, information is written
starting from the end of the file.

Use the PRINT#, PRINT# USING, and WRITE#
statements to write information to a sequential file.
These statements cause QuickBASIC to write exactly
the same information to the file as it would write to the
screen.

You may use the LINE INPUT# statement for reading
into a string entire records, up to a delimiting CR/LF.
Any attempt to read past the end of a file generates an
error. Use the EOF function to determine when the end
of a sequential file has been reached. To read all of the
information in a sequential file of unspecified length,
use the EOF function with a DO...LOOP structure to
control the reading of the file.

The following illustrates sequential file creation and
reading techniques:

```
OPEN "FILE.SEQ" FOR OUTPUT AS #1
FOR I = 1 to 10
    WRITE #1, Words$(I),
    Numbers(I)
NEXT I
CLOSE #1
OPEN "FILE.SEQ" FOR INPUT AS #1
DO UNTIL EOF(1)
    INPUT #1, Word$, Number
    PRINT Word$, Number
LOOP
CLOSE #1
```

# Random-Access Files

A random-access file consists of a series of records, all
of the same length. Generally, every record contains the
same type of information in the same format. Any record
in a random-access file may be accessed directly.

Open random-access files in random mode (the default
mode for the OPEN statement). When you open the file,
you must specify the record's length if it differs from the
default value of 128 bytes.

You may read information from and write information to
an open random-access file by using the GET and PUT
statements. User-defined data types offer a straightfor-
ward way of accessing information in a random-access
file. Use the TYPE...END TYPE statements to define
a data type that corresponds to the information to be
stored in each random-access record. Define a record
variable to be of this user-defined type. You may then
use GET and PUT with the record variable. The length of
the user-defined type must be the same (in bytes) as the
record length of the file.

Random-access files contain a pointer specifying the
next record to be accessed in the file. When a random-
access file is opened, the pointer points to the first

record. You may use the SEEK function to determine
(and also to change) the pointer's location. And you can
use the GET and PUT statements to read or write directly
to any record in a file.

The following illustrates random-access file techniques:

```
TYPE RandomType
   Word AS STRING*30
   Number AS SINGLE
END TYPE
DIM RndRec AS RandomType
OPEN "FILE.RND" AS #1 LEN=34
FOR I = 1 to 10
   RndRec.Word = Words$(I)
   RndRec.Number = Numbers(I)
   PUT #1, , RndRec
NEXT I
GET #1, 3, RndRec
PRINT RndRec.Word, RndRec.Number
CLOSE #1
```

# Binary Files

With binary file types, you can access any byte in a file.
Any file can be opened as a binary file. A file opened in
BINARY mode is viewed as a long string of bytes and
may include any bytes in any positions. A binary file has
no structure; interpreting the information is your respon-
sibility.

Binary files use a pointer in much the same way as do
random-access files, except that the pointer specifies an
individual byte (not a record) in the file. When you open
a binary file, the pointer points to the first byte. You
may use the SEEK function to determine and to change
the pointer's location. The starting byte for reading and
writing to a binary file may also be specified directly in
the GET and PUT statements.

Use the GET and PUT statements to read from and write
to a binary file. The PUT statement writes to the file all
of the bytes in a specified variable. The GET statement

reads as many bytes as will fit into the variable specified. When you use variable-length strings with GET statements, the number of bytes read from the file is equal to the string's current length.

The following illustrates binary file techniques:

```
DIM LongString AS STRING * 1000
DIM ShortString AS STRING * 10

OPEN "FILE.BIN" FOR BINARY AS #1
PUT #1, , LongString
GET #1, 200, ShortString
PRINT ShortString
CLOSE #1
```

## Memory-Image Files

A memory-image file consists of the contents of a block of memory copied into a disk file with no additional structure. You may copy back into memory the information in a memory-image file. One application of a memory-image file is to save a screen image in a disk file, as illustrated by the following code:

```
DEF SEG = &HB00
BSAVE "SCREEN.MEM", 0, 800
CLS
BLOAD "SCREEN.MEM"
```

For a CGA, change &HB00 to &HB80.

## Using Devices in Place of Disk Files

You may use input and output devices other than the disk for I/O, just like disk files. To open the devices you must use the OPEN statement, substituting the device name for that of the disk file. Then the statements for disk file input and output may be used with these devices.

The file I/O statements may be used to open the following devices for input or output.

COM1: Communications port (serial) 1
COM2: Communications port (serial) 2
CONS: Screen
KYBD: Keyboard
LPT1: Printer port (parallel) 1
LPT2: Printer port (parallel) 2
LPT3: Printer port (parallel) 3
SCRN: Screen

The devices have certain limitations. The screen and printer port devices may be used only for output, the keyboard only for input. Certain functions or operations do not make sense for certain devices. For example, you cannot use the EOF, LOC, and LOF functions with the screen, keyboard, or printer devices. Most limitations follow logically from the nature of the devices.

Device output can be used to direct output to different locations at different times, as in the following code fragment:

```
SUB PrintMessage (Location$)
    OPEN Location$ FOR OUTPUT AS #1
    PRINT #1 "This is the Message"
    CLOSE #1
END SUB

CALL PrintMessage("SCRN:")
CALL PrintMessage("LPT1:")
CALL PrintMessage("MESSAGE.OUT")
```

# BLOAD

*Statement*

### Syntax

BLOAD *file* [ , *address*]

### Purpose

Loads into memory the memory-image file specified by *file*. With no *address* specified, this statement loads the file into the location from which it was saved. With an *address*, loads the file beginning at that address offset, using either the BASIC data segment or the segment specified in the last DEF SEG statement.

# BSAVE

*Statement*

### Syntax

BSAVE *filename*, *address*, *bytes*

### Purpose

Saves a copy of a specified number of *bytes* of memory as a memory-image file specified by *file*. Area to be saved begins at *address*, offset from either the BASIC data segment as the default segment or the segment specified in the last DEF SEG statement.

# CLOSE

*Statement*

### Syntax

CLOSE [ [#] *filenum* [, [#] *filenum*]...]]

### Purpose

Closes files specified by *file number* (all files, if no *file numbers* are given). This statement writes the buffer contents to disk, if needed, and releases buffer space and file numbers.

# EOF

*Function*

### Syntax

EOF (*filenum*)

### Purpose

Determines when end-of-file for file specified by *file number* has been reached, returning *true* (–1).

# FILEATTR

*Function*

### Syntax

FILEATTR (*filenum, attrib*)

### Purpose

Determines information about the file specified by *file number*. If *n* is 1, function returns mode for which file was opened. If *n* is 2, function returns DOS file handle. Mode codes returned are

1. INPUT
2. OUTPUT
4. RANDOM
8. APPEND
32. BINARY

# FREEFILE

*Function*

### Syntax

FREEFILE

### Purpose

Determines lowest unused file number.

# GET

*Statement*

### Syntax

GET [#] *filenum* [, [*recnum*] [, *var*]]

### Purpose

Reads a record from a random-access file (or bytes from a binary file) specified by *file number*. This statement reads the record (or bytes) specified by *record number*, the record (or bytes) following the last record (or bytes) read, or the record (or bytes) specified by the last SEEK statement. If a *variable* is specified, the statement reads

information into that variable and avoids the need for a
FILED statement.

# INPUT$

*Function*

### Syntax

```
INPUT$(n, [#] filenum)
```

### Purpose

Reads *n* bytes from file specified by *file number*. For
random-access files, *n* must be less than or equal to
record length.

# INPUT#

*Statement*

### Syntax

```
INPUT #filenum, var [,var]...
```

### Purpose

Reads from sequential file specified by *file number* and
assigns the data items to *variables*. Data items read must
be compatible with variable types.

# LEN

*Function*

### Syntax

```
LEN(var)
```

### Purpose

Determines number of bytes of storage required by
*variable*.

# LINE INPUT#

*Statement*

### Syntax

    LINE INPUT #*filenum*, *strvar*

### Purpose

Reads characters up to next CR/LF from file specified
by *file number* and assigns them to *string variable*.

# LOC

*Function*

### Syntax

    LOC (*filenum*)

### Purpose

Determines for file specified by *file number* the last
record read or written (random-access file); the current
byte position divided by 128 (sequential file); or the
position of the last byte read or written (binary file).

# LOCK...UNLOCK

*Statements*

### Syntax

    LOCK [#]*filenum* [, {*recnum* | [*startnum*]
        TO *endnum*}]
      [*statements*]
    UNLOCK [#]*filenum* [, {*recnum* | [*startnum*]
        TO *endnum*}]

### Purpose

Limits access by other programs to some or all of file
specified by *file number*. You can specify a *record
number* or byte or a range of record numbers from an
optional *starting record number* to an *ending record
number* or byte to be locked. The LOCK and UNLOCK

statements must match exactly. This statement, which is intended for network applications, requires DOS V3.1 or later and use of SHARE.EXE program.

# LOF

*Function*

### Syntax

```
LOF (filenum)
```

### Purpose

Determines length (in bytes) of file specified by *file number*.

# OPEN

*Statement*

### Syntax

Version 1:

```
OPEN file [FOR mode] [ACCESS access] [lock]
        AS [#] filenum [LEN=recordlen]
```

Version 2:

```
OPEN modestr, [#] filenum, file [,recordlen]
```

### Purpose

Opens file specified by *file*, to be accessed by *file number*. In version 1, *mode* is the mode of access to be used with the file, as follows:

| | |
|---|---|
| APPEND | Sequential output with pointer at end of file |
| BINARY | Binary-byte input and output |
| INPUT | Sequential input |
| OUTPUT | Sequential output |
| RANDOM | Random-access (default mode) |

In version 2, *mode string* is a string expression. First letter of the string designates the mode, corresponding to the first letters of *modes* used with version 1. The *record length* specifies the number of bytes in a random-access record. The default is 128 bytes. You can also open various devices by substituting device name for *file*. Valid devices are

COM*n*: Communications port *n* for input and output
CONS: Console (screen) for output
KYBD: Keyboard for input only
LPT*n*: Line printer port *n* for output only
SCRN: Screen for output only

The *access* and *lock* values are relevant only when you are working in a multiuser environment. These parameters require DOS V3.1 or later and use of the SHARE.EXE program. The *access* value specifies how files are to be accessed. Options are

| READ | Reading only |
| --- | --- |
| READ WRITE | Reading and writing for RANDOM, BINARY, and APPEND files |
| WRITE | Writing only |

The *lock* values restrict access by other users, as follows:

| LOCK READ | Others may not read file |
| --- | --- |
| LOCK READ WRITE | Others may not read or write to file (default) |
| LOCK WRITE | Others may not write to file |
| SHARED | Others may read or write to file |

# PRINT #

*Statement*

### Syntax

    PRINT #filenum, [expr [{,|;} [expr]]...]

### Purpose

Writes values of *expressions* to file specified by *file number*. This file must be a sequential file opened for OUTPUT or APPEND. The statement works like the PRINT statement.

# PRINT # USING

*Statement*

### Syntax

```
PRINT # filenum, USING formatstr;
       [expr [; [expr]]...] [{,|;}]
```

### Purpose

Writes values of *expressions* to file specified by *file number*. This must be a sequential file opened for OUTPUT or APPEND. This statement works like the PRINT USING statement.

# PUT

*Statement*

### Syntax

```
PUT [#] filenum [, [recnum] [,var]]
```

### Purpose

Writes record to random-access file (or bytes to binary file) specified by *file number*. This statement writes the record (or bytes) specified by *record number*, the record (or bytes) following the last one read, or the record (or bytes) specified by last SEEK statement. If you specify a *variable*, the statement writes information from that variable, avoiding the need for a FIELD statement.

# RESET

*Statement*

### Syntax

```
RESET
```

### Purpose

Closes all files.

**SEEK**

*Function*

### Syntax

    SEEK (*filenum*)

### Purpose

Determines current position in file specified by *file number*. This position is the next record for random-access files and the next byte for all other file types.

**SEEK**

*Statement*

### Syntax

    SEEK [#]*filenum*, *pos*

### Purpose

Specifies new position in file specified by *file number*. This is position of next record for random-access files and position of next byte for all other file types. This statement has no effect on devices.

**WIDTH**

*Statement*

### Syntax

    WIDTH {#*filenum* | *dev*}, *width*

### Purpose

Specifies line width for either the file with the given *file number* or for the specified output *device*. This statement affects open files immediately; it does not affect devices until next OPEN statement.

## WRITE#

*Statement*

### Syntax

```
WRITE #filenum, [expr [, [expr]...]
```

### Purpose

Writes values of *expressions* to file specified by *file number*. Values written are separated by commas, with strings enclosed in quotation marks, in an appropriate format for reading by an INPUT# statement. File must be a sequential file opened for OUTPUT or APPEND.

# Old Random-Access Statements and Functions

Use the following statements and functions when you access random-access files by using the FIELD statement procedures rather than record variables.

## CVD

*Function*

### Syntax

```
CVD (string)
```

### Purpose

Converts an eight-byte string into a double-precision number.

## CVI

*Function*

### Syntax

```
CVI (string)
```

### Purpose

Converts a two-byte string into an integer.

# CVL

*Function*

### Syntax

CVL (*string*)

### Purpose

Converts a four-byte string into a long integer.

# CVS

*Function*

### Syntax

CVS (*string*)

### Purpose

Converts a four-byte string into a single-precision number.

# CVDMBF

*Function*

### Syntax

CVDMBF (*string*)

### Purpose

Converts an eight-byte string with a number stored in Microsoft Binary Format to a double-precision number.

# CVSMBF

*Function*

### Syntax

CVSMBF (*string*)

### Purpose

Converts a four-byte string with a number stored in Microsoft Binary Format to a single-precision number.

# FIELD

*Statement*

### Syntax

    FIELD [#]*filenum*, *width* AS *strvar*
        [,*width* AS *strvar*] . . .

### Purpose

Defines *string variable* as the means for accessing (in random-access file buffer) information for file specified by *file number*. The *width* is the width of the field in the record. The collective lengths of the strings may not exceed the record length specified for the file.

# LSET

*Statement*

### Syntax

    LSET *strvar* = *strexpr*

### Purpose

Places *string expression* left-justified in *string variable* specified in FIELD statement, filling any remaining spaces with blanks. If *string expression* is longer than current length of *string variable*, statement truncates characters from end of *string expression*. Do right-justification with RSET.

# MKD$

*Function*

### Syntax

    MKD$ (*numexpr*)

### Purpose

Converts double-precision value of *numeric expression* into an eight-byte string.

## MKI$

*Function*

### Syntax

MKI$(*numexpr*)

### Purpose

Converts integer value of *numeric expression* into a two-byte string.

## MKL$

*Function*

### Syntax

MKL$(*numexpr*)

### Purpose

Converts long integer value of *numeric expression* into a four-byte string.

## MKS$

*Function*

### Syntax

MKS$(*numexpr*)

### Purpose

Converts single-precision value of *numeric expression* into a four-byte string.

## MKDMBF$

*Function*

### Syntax

MKDMBF$(*numexpr*)

### Purpose

Converts double-precision value of *numeric expression* into an eight-byte string with the number in Microsoft Binary Format.

# MKSMBF$

*Function*

### Syntax

MKSMBF$ (*numexpr*)

### Purpose

Converts single-precision value of *numeric expression* into a four-byte string with the number in Microsoft Binary Format.

# RSET

*Statement*

### Syntax

RSET *strvar* = *strexpr*

### Purpose

Places *string expression* right-justified in the *string variable* specified in the FIELD statement, filling any remaining spaces with blanks. If *string expression* is longer than current length of *string variable*, the statement truncates characters from end of *string expression*. Do left-justification with LSET.

## Miscellaneous I/O

This section presents statements and functions used for a variety of input and output activities.

# Reading Data from within Programs

You may include constant values within a program in DATA statements. These values are assigned to variables using the READ statement.

***Statement***

### Syntax

DATA *const* [, *const*] ...

### Purpose

A DATA statement is a list of *constants* that may be assigned to variables with the READ statement. Multiple DATA statements form a continuing list. Only string constants that contain colons, commas, or leading or trailing spaces need quotation marks. If nothing is entered between two commas, the value is considered to be zero for numeric variables and null for string variables.

***Statement***

### Syntax

READ *var* [, *var*] ...

### Purpose

Assigns to *variables* the values taken from DATA statements. The first READ begins with the first DATA element and proceeds through succeeding DATA elements and statements. Subsequent READs begin where the previous READ left off, unless RESTORE has been used. Values in DATA statements must be compatible with the *variable* types.

# RESTORE

*Statement*

### Syntax

    RESTORE [lineident]

### Purpose

Causes next READ statement to begin reading values
from DATA statement specified by *line identifier*. If you
have specified no line identifier, RESTORE starts with
first DATA statement.

## Reading Data from the Command Line

The COMMAND$ function is used for reading information
entered after program name is on the command line
when starting the program as an .EXE file.

# COMMAND$

*Function*

### Syntax

    COMMAND$

### Purpose

Yields a string that is the information typed on command line after the program name when program was
invoked as an .EXE program. When working within the
QuickBASIC environment, you can set the value to be
returned by using **Modify COMMAND$**

## Reading the Date, Time, and Timer

With the following functions, you can read the system
date and time.

# DATE$

*Function*

### Syntax

DATE$

### Purpose

Returns a string with current system date in the form
*mm-dd-yyyy*.

# TIME$

*Function*

### Syntax

TIME$

### Purpose

Returns a string with current system time in the form
*hh:mm:ss*.

# TIMER

*Function*

### Syntax

TIMER

### Purpose

Determines number of seconds since midnight, based on
system clock.

## Graphics

To output graphics, you must first use the SCREEN
statement to specify a graphics mode. You may optionally use PALETTE and COLOR statements to specify
colors. Several statements then may be used to modify
the graphics environment.

# The Graphics Environment

Use the WINDOW statement to specify a logical coordinate system for drawing graphics. Use VIEW to specify a portion of the screen as a viewport to which QuickBASIC will restrict the drawing of graphics.

# PMAP

*Function*

### Syntax

PMAP (*numexpr, n*)

### Purpose

Determines associated physical and logical coordinates. The *numeric expression* is the coordinate value. If *n* is 1, assumes *numeric expression* is the logical horizontal coordinate and returns the physical horizontal coordinate. If *n* is 2, performs same action for the vertical coordinate. If *n* is 3, assumes *numeric expression* is the physical horizontal coordinate and returns the logical horizontal coordinate. If *n* is 4, the function performs same action for the vertical coordinate.

# POINT

*Function*

### Syntax

POINT (*hor, vert*)
POINT (*n*)

### Purpose

The function's first form determines color number of point specified by coordinates *horizontal* and *vertical*. The second form determines position of graphics cursor. If *n* is 0, the function returns physical horizontal coordinate; if *n* is 1, returns physical vertical coordinate. Values for *n* of 2 and 3 give logical horizontal and vertical coordinates, respectively.

# VIEW

*Statement*

## Syntax

```
VIEW [[SCREEN] (hor1, vert1) - (hor2, vert2)
    [,[color] [,border]]]
```

## Purpose

Specifies section of graphics screen as viewport. Drawing of graphics is limited to this viewport. You define the viewport by specifying the coordinates of two diagonally opposite corners, *horizontal 1*, *vertical 1* and *horizontal 2*, *vertical 2*. Coordinates in graphics drawing statements are relative to upper left corner of viewport unless SCREEN option is specified, in which case coordinates will be relative to entire screen. If you specify *color*, viewport is filled with specified color. If you specify *border*, QuickBASIC will draw a line around viewport in color specified by *border*. With no arguments, the statement resets viewport to entire screen.

# WINDOW

*Statement*

## Syntax

```
WINDOW [[SCREEN] (hor1, vert1) -
    (hor2, vert2)]
```

## Purpose

Defines a logical coordinate system to be used for drawing to the screen, specified by the coordinates for two diagonally opposite corners, *horizontal 1*, *vertical 1* and *horizontal 2*, *vertical 2*. The SCREEN option inverts the direction of the vertical axis to increase from bottom to top, as with normal Cartesian coordinates. Values must be single-precision numbers. With no arguments, the statement resets the coordinate system to the physical coordinates for screen mode.

# Drawing Graphics

Statements for drawing graphics use either the logical coordinate system as specified by a WINDOW statement or the physical coordinates associated with a screen mode. If you have used the VIEW statement to specify a portion of the screen as a viewport, QuickBASIC will limit graphics drawing to this area.

# CIRCLE

*Statement*

### Syntax

```
CIRCLE [STEP] (hor, vert), rad
        [, [color] [, [arcbegin] [, [arcend]
        [, aspect] ] ] ]
```

### Purpose

Draws a circle with its center at the specified *horizontal* and *vertical* coordinates with the *radius* specified. If STEP is included, *horizontal* and *vertical* are offsets from the graphics cursor position. Draws in foreground color or optional *color*. CIRCLE draws an arc if you specify *arcbegin* and *arcend*, in radians. *Aspect* is ratio of vertical to horizontal radius.

# DRAW

*Statement*

### Syntax

```
DRAW strexpr
```

### Purpose

Draws on graphics screen following commands included in *string expression*. The following commands move graphics cursor and draw:

| | |
|---|---|
| U [n] | Go up *n* units. |
| D [n] | Go down *n* units. |

| | |
|---|---|
| L [*n*] | Go left *n* units. |
| R [*n*] | Go right *n* units. |
| E [*n*] | Go up *n* units and right *n* units on the diagonal. |
| F [*n*] | Go down *n* units and right *n* units on the diagonal. |
| G [*n*] | Go down *n* units and left *n* units on the diagonal. |
| H [*n*] | Go up *n* units and left *n* units on the diagonal. |
| M *hor, vert* | Go to position specified by *horizontal* and *vertical* coordinates. |
| M+ *hor, vert* | Go to position specified by adding *horizontal* and *vertical* to current position. |
| M- *hor, vert* | Go to position specified by subtracting *horizontal* and *vertical* from current position. |

If one of the following commands is made a prefix to any of the preceding commands, the action changes as specified:

| | |
|---|---|
| B | Do not draw; move cursor only. |
| N | Draw; return cursor to starting position when done. |

The following optional commands change the manner in which the drawing takes place:

| | |
|---|---|
| A *n* | Rotate directions of commands according to value of *n*: 0 for 0 degrees, 1 for 90 degrees, 2 for 180 degrees, 3 for 270 degrees; scales figures to same size for all angles. |
| C *col* | Change drawing *color*. |
| P *col1, col2* | Specify *color 1* as paint color for interior and *color 2* as color for border. |

| | |
|---|---|
| S *n* | Specify a scale factor of *n* (0 to 255) which is multiplied by units in movement commands to determine number of pixels moved. |
| TA *n* | Rotate directions of commands by *n* degrees (–360 to 360). |
| V | Use logical coordinates for all the following DRAW commands. |
| X *strexpr* | Use commands in the *string expression*. |

To use variables as the arguments for any of the commands, you must use the VARPTR$ function. For example, use "U" + VARPTR$(A) to move up by A units and "X" + VARPTR$(B$) to use the commands in the string B$.

***Statement***

### Syntax

GET [STEP] (*hor1, vert1*) - [STEP]
        (*hor2, vert2*) , *array* [ (*arrayindices*) ]

### Purpose

Copies a graphics image from screen into a numeric array for later use with PUT command. The coordinates *horizontal 1*, *vertical 1*, and *horizontal 2*, *vertical 2* are opposite corners of the area to be copied. The first STEP keyword makes these positions relative to the current position of the graphics cursor; the second STEP makes the second set of coordinates relative to the first. Use optional *array indices* to specify that storage of the image is to begin with a specific element.

# LINE

### *Statement*

## Syntax

```
LINE [[STEP](hor1, vert1)]-[STEP]
        (hor2, vert2)[,[color][,[B[F]]
     [,linemask]]]
```

## Purpose

Draws line from coordinates *horizontal 1*, *vertical 1* to
coordinates *horizontal 2*, *vertical 2*. If first set of
coordinates is not specified, statement draws a line from
current graphics cursor position. If STEP is specified,
coordinates are relative to last specified cursor position.
This statement draws either in foreground color or in
optional *color*. B draws a box with coordinate pairs as
opposite corners; BF also fills box with specified color.
The *linemask* is an optional integer value to draw dotted
lines. The bits in *linemask* determine whether a point is
plotted (bit equals 1) or not plotted (bit equals 0). Bits
are read from most-significant to least-significant bit and
repeated for each 16 points plotted.

# PAINT

### *Statement*

## Syntax

```
PAINT [STEP]  (hor, vert)
        [,[{color1 | patternstr}]  [,[color2]
        [,backgroundstr]]]
```

## Purpose

Fills area inside or outside of a closed figure, beginning
at coordinates specified by *horizontal* and *vertical*.
STEP makes coordinates relative to current graphics
cursor position. Fills figure with foreground color or
with optional *color 1*, stopping at a border that is
foreground color or at a border of *color 2*, if specified.
The *pattern string* can have up to 64 characters. Each

character defines an 8-bit horizontal pattern for which color is turned on if bit is 1 and off if bit is 0. Successive characters represent patterns below first pattern. To paint over an area previously painted with a one- or two-character pattern string, specify the original pattern string as the background string. In this way, you prevent the previous pattern from being interpreted as a border, thereby stopping the painting operation.

# PRESET

*Statement*

### Syntax

```
PRESET [STEP] (hor, vert) [,color]
```

### Purpose

Draws point at coordinates specified by *horizontal* and *vertical*. PRESET draws with background color or with *color*, if specified.

# PSET

*Statement*

### Syntax

```
PSET [STEP] (hor, vert) [,color]
```

### Purpose

Draws point at coordinates specified by *horizontal* and *vertical*. PSET draws with foreground color or with *color*, if specified.

# PUT

*Statement*

### Syntax

```
PUT [STEP] (hor, vert), array[(arrayindices)]
    [,drawoption]
```

## Purpose

Draws image copied into *array* with GET statement,
with *horizontal* and *vertical* coordinates specifying the
image's upper left corner. The optional *array indices*
specify that image begins at that element in the array.
The *draw option* specifies how this image is to be drawn
in relation to existing image on-screen. A list of the
options (XOR is the default) follows:

AND              Bit-wise logical AND of screen image
and stored image. When point in
screen image and stored image both
have same color, then point is given
that color; otherwise not.

OR               Bit-wise logical OR of screen image
and stored image. When point in
either screen image or stored image
has a color, then point is given that
color; otherwise not.

PSET           Draws image exactly as captured by
GET. This option ignores existing
screen image.

PRESET       Draws inverse of image captured by
GET, reversing value of each bit, to
produce a negative image

XOR             Bit-wise logical XOR of screen image
and stored image. Reverses bits in
screen image. Repeating PUT
command using XOR restores
original image.

# Sound Output

Use the following statements to produce sounds from the
speaker.

**BEEP**

*Statement*

### Syntax
    BEEP

### Purpose
Produces a sound through the speaker. This sound is the same as that produced by printing CHR$(7).

**PLAY**

*Function*

### Syntax
    PLAY (*numexpr*)

### Purpose
Determines number of notes in background music queue. *Numexpr* may have any value.

**PLAY**

*Statement*

### Syntax
    PLAY *strexpr*

### Purpose
Plays music following the commands included in *string expression*, as follows:

| | |
|---|---|
| A–G | Play note in current octave |
| # or + | Following note, make note sharp |
| – | Following note, make note flat |
| N *n* | Play note for *n*, 0 to 84; 0 is rest |
| o *n* | Set octave for *n*, 0 to 6 |
| > | Switch to next higher octave |
| < | Switch to next lower octave |

| L n | Play notes with duration n, 1 to 64; 1 is whole note, 2 half, 4 quarter, etc. |
| P *n* | Pause for duration *n*, 1 to 64, in units specified by L |
| . | After note, play note 1.5 times current duration L |
| T *n* | Play tempo *n* quarter notes per minute; range 32 to 255, default 120 |
| MB | Play music in background (maximum 32 notes) |
| MF | Play music in foreground (default) |
| ML | Play legato; note plays entire duration L |
| MN | Play normal; note plays 7/8 of duration L |
| MS | Play staccato; note plays 3/4 duration L |
| X *strexpr* | Use commands in *string expression* |

To use variables as the arguments for any of the commands, you must use the VARPTR$ function. For example, use "L=" + VARPTR$(A) to play notes with duration A, and "X" + VARPTR$(B$) to use the commands in the string B$.

# SOUND

*Statement*

### Syntax

SOUND *freq*, *dur*

### Purpose

Produces a sound with the frequency in hertz specified by *frequency* (37–32,767) and with the length in clock ticks specified by *duration* (0–65,535, with 18.2 clock ticks per second). A *duration* of zero turns off a sound that is being produced.

# Communications Port I/O

To read from and write to a communications (serial)
port, you must open the device by using a special form
of the OPEN statement. After opening a communications
port, you handle input and output operations by using
the commands appropriate for any file or device.

# OPEN COM

*Statement*

### Syntax

```
OPEN "COMn: [speed] [,parity] [, [data]
      [, [stop] [,option]...]]]]]"
      [FOR mode] AS [#] filenum
      [LEN=recordlen]
```

### Purpose

This statement is a special form of the OPEN statement
for opening communications port *n* as the file specified
by *file number*. The *speed* is baud rate. The *parity* is N
for none, E for even, O for odd, S for space, and M for
mark. The *data* is the number of data bits, 5, 6, 7, or 8.
*Stop* is the number of stop bits, 1, 5, or 2. You may
specify any of the following *options*:

| | |
|---|---|
| ASC | Operate in ASCII mode |
| BIN | Operate in binary mode (default) |
| CD [*n*] | Sets device timeout for Carrier-Detect line to *n* milliseconds |
| CS [*n*] | Sets device timeout for Clear-To-Send line to *n* milliseconds |
| DS [*n*] | Sets device timeout for Data-Set-Ready line to *n* milliseconds |
| LF | Inserts line-feed character after carriage-return character for printing |
| OP [*n*] | Sets timeout for OPEN statement to find communications line active to *n* milliseconds |

| RB [n] | Sets receive buffer size to n bytes |
| RS | Ignore Request to Send line |
| TB [n] | Sets transmit buffer size to n bytes |

The *mode* must be INPUT, OUTPUT, or RANDOM. When mode is RANDOM, use *record length* to set size of random-access buffer in bytes.

# Joystick and Light Pen Input

Use the following functions to read joystick and light pen status.

*Function*

### Syntax

PEN (n)

### Purpose

Determines information from light pen, where *n* specifies information returned:

0   Use since last check: −1 if used, 0 if not
1   Horizontal pixel coordinate of last pen press
2   Vertical pixel coordinate of last pen press
3   Pen switch: −1 if down, 0 if up
4   Last valid horizontal pixel coordinate known
5   Last valid vertical pixel coordinate known
6   Character line position of last pen press
7   Character column position of last pen press
8   Last valid character line position known
9   Last valid character column position known

*Function*

### Syntax

STICK (n)

### Purpose

Determines joystick positions. If *n* is 0, the function returns *x* coordinate of joystick A from 1 to 200; if *n* is 1, the function returns *y* coordinate. If *n* is 2 or 3, the function returns *x* or *y* coordinate of joystick B. STICK(0) must be executed first to read all joystick coordinates as well as to return *x* coordinate of A.

## STRIG

*Function*

### Syntax

    STRIG(n)

### Purpose

Determines the pressing of joystick buttons. Returns *true* (−1) for the following values of *n* and conditions:

| | |
|---|---|
| 0 | Lower A button pressed since last STRIG(0) |
| 1 | Lower A button now pressed |
| 2 | Lower B button pressed since last STRIG(2) |
| 3 | Lower B button now pressed |
| 4 | Upper A button pressed since last STRIG(4) |
| 5 | Upper A button now pressed |
| 6 | Upper B button pressed since last STRIG(6) |
| 7 | Upper B button now pressed |

## STRIG

*Statement*

### Syntax

    STRIG {ON | OFF}

### Purpose

Used in previous versions of BASIC but ignored by QuickBASIC.

# Microprocessor Port Input and Output

You may read bytes from and write them to any micro-processor port by using these statements and functions.

*Function*

### Syntax

INP (*port*)

### Purpose

Reads a byte (integer) from the specified *port*, which must be an integer ranging from 0 to 65,535.

*Statement*

### Syntax

OUT *port*, *numexpr*

### Purpose

Sends a byte to the specified *port*, which must be an integer ranging from 0 to 65,535. The *numexpr* must have an integer value from 0 to 255.

*Statement*

### Syntax

WAIT *port*, *numexpr1* [, *numexpr2*]

### Purpose

Pauses until a byte with a specified bit pattern is read from specified *port*. This statement reads a byte from the port, performs an XOR of the byte with *numeric expression 2*, and performs an AND of the result with *numeric expression 1*. This statement rereads bytes from the port until the result is nonzero. The *numeric expressions* must have integer values. If *numeric expression 2* is omitted, *numeric expression* is assumed to be zero.

# Device Driver Control

You may determine and alter the status of a device driver. You must have used the OPEN statement to open the device, and the device driver must process IOCTL strings.

## IOCTL$

*Function*

### Syntax

```
IOCTL$([#]filenum)
```

### Purpose

Reads a string with control data from the device driver for file or device specified by file number.

## IOCTL

*Statement*

### Syntax

```
IOCTL [#] filenum, strexpr
```

### Purpose

Sends string with control data to device driver for the file or device specified by *file number*.

# Miscellaneous Statements and Functions

QuickBASIC includes statements and functions for event trapping, error handling, performing DOS-related functions, dealing with memory, chaining to other programs, and calling routines in other languages.

# Event Trapping

QuickBASIC can detect when specified events occur and then transfer control to a subroutine to respond to the event. The program must first execute an ON *event* statement to specify the location of the subroutine to which control is to be transferred. Then the program must execute an *event* ON statement to enable event trapping. When you are compiling programs with event trapping from the DOS prompt, use the /v or /w options with the bc command.

**Statement**

### Syntax
COM(*n*) {ON | OFF | STOP}

### Purpose
Controls event trapping on communications port *n*. The event is the arrival of a character at the port. ON enables and OFF disables event trapping; STOP turns off trapping but saves events for the next ON.

**Statement**

### Syntax
KEY *n*, *strexpr*

### Purpose
Defines keystroke combination *n* for event trapping where *n* is from 15 to 25. The *string expression* is a two-character string where first character has the value of the keyboard flag and second character has the value of the

keyboard scan code. You can use the CHR$ function to create a string with those values.

The decimal values for the keyboard flags are

| Value | Key |
|-------|-----|
| 0 | No flag |
| 1,2,3 | Shift |
| 4 | Ctrl |
| 8 | Alt |
| 32 | NumLock |
| 64 | CapsLock |
| 128 | Extended keys on 101-key keyboard |

The decimal values for the scan codes are

| Value | Key | | Value | Key |
|-------|-----|---|-------|-----|
| 1 | Esc | | 36 | J |
| 2 | 1 ! | | 37 | K |
| 3 | 2 @ | | 38 | L |
| 4 | 3 # | | 39 | ; : |
| 5 | 4 $ | | 40 | ' " |
| 6 | 5 % | | 41 | ` ~ |
| 7 | 6 ^ | | 42 | Left Shift |
| 8 | 7 & | | 43 | \ | |
| 9 | 8 * | | 44 | Z |
| 10 | 9 ( | | 45 | X |
| 11 | 0 ) | | 46 | C |
| 12 | + _ | | 47 | V |
| 13 | = + | | 48 | B |
| 14 | Left | | 49 | N |
| 15 | Tab | | 50 | M |
| 16 | Q | | 51 | , < |
| 17 | W | | 52 | . > |
| 18 | E | | 53 | / ? |
| 19 | R | | 54 | Right Shift |
| 20 | T | | 55 | * PrtScr |
| 21 | Y | | 56 | Alt |
| 22 | U | | 57 | Space |
| 23 | I | | 58 | CapsLock |
| 24 | O | | 59 | F1 |
| 25 | P | | 60 | F2 |
| 26 | [ { | | 61 | F3 |
| 27 | ] } | | 62 | F4 |
| 28 | Enter | | 63 | F5 |
| 29 | Ctrl | | 64 | F6 |
| 30 | A | | 65 | F7 |
| 31 | S | | 66 | F8 |
| 32 | D | | 67 | F9 |
| 33 | F | | 68 | F10 |
| 34 | G | | 69 | NumLock |
| 35 | H | | 70 | Scroll Lock |

| *Value* | *Key* | *Value* | *Key* |
|---------|-------|---------|-------|
| 71 | Home 7 | 78 | Grey + |
| 72 | Up 8 | 79 | End 1 |
| 73 | PgUp 9 | 80 | Down 2 |
| 74 | Grey + | 81 | PgDn 3 |
| 75 | Left 4 | 82 | Ins 0 |
| 76 | Center 5 | 83 | Del . |
| 77 | Right 6 | 84 | Shift |

# KEY(n)

*Statement*

### Syntax

```
KEY(n) {ON | OFF | STOP}
```

### Purpose

Controls event trapping on key specified by *n*. The event is pressing of key. ON enables event trapping; OFF disables event trapping; STOP turns off trapping but saves events for next ON. The values of *n* refer to the following keys:

| 1–10 | Function keys F1 to F10 |
|-------|-------------------------|
| 11 | ↑ |
| 12 | ← |
| 13 | → |
| 14 | ↓ |
| 13–25 | User-defined keys set with KEY |
| 30–31 | Functions keys F11 and F12 |

# ON *event* GOSUB

*Statement*

### Syntax

```
ON event GOSUB lineident
```

### Purpose

Transfers control to the subroutine beginning with statement identified by *line identifier*, either a line number or a label, when a specified *event* occurs. The *events* are

| COM(n) | Character arrival at communications port n |
| KEY(n) | Pressing of key n; see KEY(n) statements |
| PEN | Light pen activation |
| PLAY(n) | Number of notes in music buffer dropping below n |
| STRIG(n) | Pressing of joystick button n; see STRIG(n) |
| TIMER(n) | Passage of n seconds where n is 1 to 86,400 |

Use the RETURN statement to end an event-induced subroutine.

*Statement*

#### Syntax

```
PEN {ON | OFF | STOP}
```

#### Purpose

Controls event trapping for light pen. The event is the pen's activation. ON enables event trapping; OFF disables event trapping; STOP turns off trapping but saves events for next ON.

*Statement*

#### Syntax

```
PLAY {ON | OFF | STOP}
```

#### Purpose

Controls event trapping of play events. The event is the number of notes in music buffer dropping below level specified in the ON PLAY statement. ON enables and OFF disables event trapping; STOP turns off trapping but saves events for next ON.

# STRIG

*Statement*

### Syntax

```
STRIG(n) {ON | OFF | STOP}
```

### Purpose

Controls event trapping of joystick button pressing. The event is the pressing of joystick button specified by *n*, where 0 is lower button on A, 2 is lower button on B, 4 is upper button on A, 6 is upper button on B. ON enables and OFF disables event trapping; STOP turns off trapping but saves events for next ON.

# TIMER

*Statement*

### Syntax

```
TIMER {ON | OFF | STOP}
```

### Purpose

Controls event trapping based on elapsed time. The event is passage of number of seconds specified in the ON TIMER statement. ON enables and OFF disables event trapping; STOP turns off trapping but saves events for next ON.

## Error Handling

You can use an error-handling routine to trap run-time errors that would otherwise result in program termination. To transfer control to an error-handling routine that will respond to the errors, you must execute an ON ERROR statement. To determine the nature of the error, various error functions may be used in the routine. Use the RESUME statement to return from the routine to the program. When you compile programs with an error-handling routine from the DOS prompt, use the /e or /x options with the **bc** command.

# ERDEV

*Function*

### Syntax

ERDEV

### Purpose

Determines error code from device with last error. This function returns an integer. The lower byte is the DOS error code; the upper byte is the device-attribute word.

# ERDEV$

*Function*

### Syntax

ERDEV$

### Purpose

Returns a string containing the name of device with last error.

# ERL

*Function*

### Syntax

ERL

### Purpose

Determines line number for line at which error occurred. This function returns an integer. ERL does not return line labels. If line has no line number, ERL returns last line number before line at which error occurred. If program has no line numbers, ERL returns zero.

# ERR

*Function*

### Syntax

ERR

#### Purpose

Determines error code for last error. This function returns an integer. A list of run-time error codes is included later in this quick reference.

# ERROR

*Statement*

#### Syntax

ERROR *numexpr*

#### Purpose

Generates error with the code specified by *numeric expression*, which must be an integer in the range 0 to 255. If value of *numeric expression* is an error code, this statement simulates occurrence of that error.

# ON ERROR GOTO

*Statement*

#### Syntax

ON ERROR GOTO *lineident*

#### Purpose

Causes control to be transferred to line specified by *line identifier* (the first line of an error-handling routine). A line number of 0 turns off error handling. When executed with a line number of 0 within an error-handling routine, statement terminates program and prints error message for error that caused entry of routine. Requires that you use option /e when compiling a program using bc from DOS command line.

# RESUME

*Statement*

#### Syntax

RESUME [{0 | NEXT | *lineident*}]

***Purpose***

Transfers execution back from error-handling routine to statement that caused error. The NEXT option transfers execution to statement after the one that caused error. Specification of *line identifier* causes execution to be transferred to line specified. Use of NEXT option requires that you use compiler option /x when compiling program using **bc** from DOS command line.

## *DOS-Related Statements and Functions*

The commands in this section perform various DOS operations and allow the calling of DOS interrupts. For more information, see your DOS reference materials or the following Que books:

❏ *DOS Programmer's Reference*

❏ *Using Assembly Language*

❏ *Using PC DOS*, 2nd Edition

# CALL INTERRUPT
*Statement*

***Syntax***

```
CALL INTERRUPT (intnum, regsin, regsout)
CALL INTERRUPTX (intnum, regsin, regsout)
```

***Purpose***

Performs DOS system call to specified interrupt. The *interrupt number* (the decimal value of the interrupt being called) must be an integer value from 0 to 255. The *registers in* are the values placed in the registers when interrupt is called. The *registers out* are the values in the registers on return from interrupt. Both *registers in* and *registers out* must be variables of the user-defined type RegType, defined as follows:

```
TYPE RegType
    AX    AS INTEGER
    BX    AS INTEGER
    CX    AS INTEGER
    DX    AS INTEGER
    BP    AS INTEGER
    SI    AS INTEGER
    DI    AS INTEGER
    FLAGS AS INTEGER
    DS    AS INTEGER
    ES    AS INTEGER
END TYPE
```

You place the register values into a variable defined to
be of RegType and use this variable for *registers in* .
To return the register values from the interrupt, another
variable defined to be of RegType is used for *registers
out*. The values in the DS and ES registers are used in
INTERRUPTX. To use the current values, set the DS
and ES values to –1 in the *registers in* variable. This
command is a routine in the Quicklibrary QB.QLB,
which you must use to make the command available.

# CALL INT86OLD

*Statement*

### Syntax

```
CALL INT86OLD (intnum, arrayin(),
    arrayout())
CALL INT86XOLD (intnum, arrayin(),
    arrayout())
```

### Purpose

Performs DOS system call to specified interrupt. This
statement is provided for compatibility with previous
INT86 and INT86X statements. This statement
performs same operations as CALL INTERRUPT
statements but uses integer arrays rather than user-
defined RegType variables for register values.
INT86XOLD statement uses 10-element arrays with
registers in same order as in RegType for both *array in*

and *array out*. INT86OLD statement uses eight-element arrays, dropping the elements for the DS and ES registers. This command is a routine in Quicklibrary QB.QLB, which you must use to make the command available.

# CHDIR

*Statement*

### Syntax
CHDIR *strexpr*

### Purpose
Changes default directory to the path specification in *string expression*. This statement works essentially like the DOS **CHDIR** (**CD**) command.

# DATE$

*Statement*

### Syntax
DATE$ = *strexpr*

### Purpose
Sets system date. The *string expression* must be in the form *mm-dd-yy*, *mm-dd-yyyy*, *mm/dd/yy*, or *mm/dd/yyyy*. The DATE$ function returns system date. This statement is similar to DOS **DATE** command.

# ENVIRON$

*Function*

### Syntax
ENVIRON$ ({*strvar* | *n*})

### Purpose
Returns string from DOS environment-string table. If you specify name of string with a *string variable*,

function returns the characters following the equal sign. If you specify a number *n*, function returns *nth* string in table, including the name and the equal sign.

# ENVIRON

**Statement**

### Syntax

ENVIRON *strexpr*
    *strexpr = parameterid{=| } text*

### Purpose

Adds or modifies parameter in DOS environment-string table as specified by *string expression*. DOS *parameterid* may be separated from *text* by an equal sign or a space. Change to DOS environment-string table lasts only for execution of current program.

# FILES

**Statement**

### Syntax

FILES [*strexpr*]

### Purpose

Prints name of files on disk as specified by *string expression* (a DOS file specification, which may include disk drive, directories, and file name or wildcards). With no string expression, statement prints names of all files in current disk and directory. FILES works essentially like DOS **DIR** /**W** command.

# KILL

**Statement**

### Syntax

KILL *strexpr*

### Purpose

Erases from disk the file(s) specified by *string expression*. The *string expression*, a DOS file specification, may include disk drive, directories, and file name or wildcards. This statement works essentially like DOS **DEL** and **ERASE** commands.

# MKDIR

*Statement*

### Syntax

```
MKDIR strexpr
```

### Purpose

Creates new directory, as specified by *string expression* (a DOS path name, which may include disk drive, directories, and name of directory to be created). This statement works essentially like the DOS **MKDIR** (**MD**) command.

# NAME

*Statement*

### Syntax

```
NAME strexpr1 AS strexpr2
```

### Purpose

Renames a file, where *string expression 1* specifies file to be renamed and may include disk drive and directories, and *string expression 2* is new file name. If *string expression 2* includes path specification for a different directory, command moves and renames file. This statement is similar to DOS **RENAME** command.

*Statement*

### Syntax

RMDIR *strexpr*

### Purpose

Removes directory from disk as specified by *string expression*. The *string expression* is a DOS path name, which may include disk drive, directories, and name of directory to be removed. Directory to be removed may not contain any stored files. This statement works essentially like DOS **RMDIR ( RD)** command.

*Statement*

### Syntax

SHELL [*strexpr*]

### Purpose

Temporarily exits to DOS to allow running of DOS commands and other programs. With no *string expression* specified, statement loads COMMAND.COM and leaves you at DOS prompt. To return to BASIC program, type **EXIT** at DOS prompt. If *string expression* specifies an executable file, SHELL executes this file and returns to program when execution is completed.

# SYSTEM

*Statement*

### Syntax

SYSTEM

### Purpose

Causes normal termination of program execution, closing all files. If program is an .EXE file executed from DOS command line, or if it was executed with the

qb /run option, SYSTEM returns to DOS. If program
was run from within QuickBASIC, SYSTEM returns to
QuickBASIC environment.

# TIME$

*Statement*

### Syntax
TIME$ = *strexpr*

### Purpose
Sets system time. The *string expression* must be in the
form *hh*, *hh:mm*, or *hh:mm:ss*. TIME$ function returns
system time. This statement is similar to the DOS **TIME**
command.

# Memory-Related Statements and Functions

With these statements, you can access values stored in
any memory location, return pointers with the addresses
at which variables are stored in memory, and control
memory allocation to a program.

# CLEAR

*Statement*

### Syntax
CLEAR [,, *stack*]

### Purpose
Sets variables to zero or null, closes files, and initializes
stack. If *stack* value is given, CLEAR allocates stack
space for the program. The latter technique is used when
an Out of stack space error is reported,
generally when you are using recursive or deeply-nested
procedures.

# DEF SEG

*Statement*

### Syntax

    DEF SEG [= address]

### Purpose

Specifies segment *address* for statements referring to
memory addresses. If *address* is not given, statement
specifies BASIC data segment.

# FRE

*Function*

### Syntax

    FRE (numexpr | strexpr)

### Purpose

Determines amount of memory available in bytes. If
*numeric expression* is –1, function returns size of largest
numeric array that could be used. If *numeric expression*
is –2, function returns amount of unused stack space.
Any other *numeric expression* returns size of next free
block for string storage. Any *string expression* returns
size of available string storage after compacting string
storage.

# PEEK

*Function*

### Syntax

    PEEK (addr)

### Purpose

Determines the byte stored in memory at specified
*address* in segment specified by DEF SEG statement.
Function returns an integer in the range 0 to 255.

# POKE
*Statement*

### Syntax
```
POKE addr, numexpr
```

### Purpose
Stores byte value of *numeric expression* (from 0 to 255) in memory at specified *address* in segment specified by DEF SEG statement.

# SADD
*Function*

### Syntax
```
SADD (strvar)
```

### Purpose
Determines address at which *string variable* is stored. Address is a two-byte integer offset from default data segment.

# SETMEM
*Function*

### Syntax
```
SETMEM (numexpr)
```

### Purpose
Increases or decreases number of bytes allocated to far heap by value of *numeric expression*. Function returns number of bytes in far heap after modification.

# VARPTR$
*Function*

### Syntax
```
VARPTR$ (var)
```

### Purpose

Determines address at which a variable is stored.

# VARPTR

*Function*

### Syntax

VARPTR (*var*)

### Purpose

Determines address at which *variable* is stored or at which string descriptor is stored for string variables. Address is a two-byte integer offset. Segment is determined with VARSEG function.

# VARSEG

*Function*

### Syntax

VARSEG (*var*)

### Purpose

Determines segment in which *variable* is stored or at which string descriptor is stored for string variables. Segment is a two-byte integer. Offset within segment is determined with VARPTR function.

## Chaining to Other BASIC Programs

With the CHAIN command, you can have a BASIC program load and execute another BASIC program. You can use CHAIN to break large programs into smaller pieces. Use COMMON statement to specify variables to be retained when you chain to a second program.

# CHAIN

*Statement*

### Syntax

```
CHAIN file
```

### Purpose

Loads and executes program specified by *file*, which may include drive and directory specifications. Within the QuickBASIC environment, this statement requires a BASIC source program and assumes .BAS extension if not specified. You may pass variables to chained program by using COMMON. When you create .EXE files for chaining programs using COMMON, use default BRUN40.LIB because BCOM40.LIB does not support use of COMMON with CHAIN.

# COMMON

*Statement*

### Syntax

```
COMMON [SHARED] [/blockname/]
        var[()] [ AS type] [, var[()]
    [AS type]]...
```

### Purpose

Establishes a block of *variables* for passing to another program when chaining or for sharing with other modules. Names of *variables* to be included in COMMON block are listed, with empty parentheses following array names. You may declare variable *type* by including AS *type* clause after variable name. All variable types are allowed. The optional SHARED keyword specifies that variables are to be shared with all SUB and FUNCTION procedures in the module. The optional blockname is a BASIC identifier used to give a name to particular COMMON block to control sharing. COMMON statement must appear before any executable statements in a module.

To share a block of variables across modules or from one program to a chained program, you must include comparable COMMON statements in both modules. Variables in the two COMMON statements must be in same order and must be of same type. Variable names, however, need not match. You may use named COMMON blocks to specify different sets of variables to be shared with different modules. Any variable may appear in only one COMMON block, however. Only an unnamed COMMON may be used to preserve variables when you are chaining to another program.

# RUN

*Statement*

## Syntax

```
RUN  [ { linenum, file } ]
```

## Purpose

Within QuickBASIC environment, RUN or RUN *linenum* begins execution of program currently in memory, either from beginning or from specified *line number*. When you specify a *file*, that program is loaded and executed. Within QuickBASIC environment, .BAS source code is loaded and executed. Otherwise an .EXE file is loaded and executed. In programs compiled using bc, RUN can load and execute .EXE files created using other languages.

# Calling Routines in Other Languages

You can easily use routines written in other languages with QuickBASIC programs. You may write routines in any of the Microsoft languages, such as C, Macro Assembler, Pascal, FORTRAN or in other languages compatible with Microsoft languages. Detailed information about this topic is beyond the scope of a quick reference. For more information, refer to Que's books

*DOS Programmer's Reference* and *Using Assembly Language*.

# CALL

***Statement***

### Syntax
Version 1:
```
CALL name [([[{BYVAL | SEG}]arg]
        [,[{BYVAL | SEG}]arg]...)]
```

Version 2:
```
name [{BYVAL | SEG}]arg]
        [,[{BYVAL | SEG}]arg]...]
```

Version 3:
```
CALLS name [([arg [,arg]...)]
```

### Purpose
Transfers execution to procedure *name* written in another language. The *arguments* are variables or constants being passed to procedure. In versions 1 and 2, default is to pass near reference to location of argument. Specifying BYVAL before an argument passes argument by value. Specifying SEG before an argument passes far reference as a segmented address. In version 3, all arguments are passed with far reference. Specify array variables by appending empty parentheses. You can use version 2 without the CALL keyword only if you have used a DECLARE statement to declare procedure.

# CALL ABSOLUTE

***Statement***

### Syntax
```
CALL ABSOLUTE ([arg [,arg]... ,] intvar)
```

### Purpose
Transfers execution to a machine-language procedure, with execution beginning at address specified by *integer*

*variable*. This address is an offset from current segment. Arguments are passed to the procedure as near pointers (offset addresses) from current segment.

# DECLARE

Statement

### Syntax

```
DECLARE {FUNCTION | SUB} name [CDECL]
      [ALIAS "aliasname"]
      [([[{BYVAL | SEG}] arg [AS type]
      [,[{BYVAL | SEG}] arg [AS type]]
      ...)]
```

### Purpose

Declares procedure *name* written in another language. Specify FUNCTION or SUB depending on whether procedure returns a value. The CDECL option specifies that arguments are to be passed in reverse order for procedures written in C and that *name* is to be converted to follow C conventions. Use ALIAS option to specify that actual name of procedure is *alias name* and that name differs from BASIC procedure *name*. List of arguments is as in CALL statement, with additional option of specifying variable *type* for each *argument*, where *type* is any elementary or user-defined type.

# *Metacommands*

QuickBASIC includes three metacommands used to specify the manner in which QuickBASIC processes programs. Unlike BASIC statements and functions, you enter these metacommands as part of a comment statement in the program, following either a REM or an apostrophe. You can enter multiple metacommands, separated by spaces, within one comment.

# $DYNAMIC

*Metacommand*

### Syntax

```
REM $DYNAMIC
```

### Purpose

Instructs BASIC to allocate memory for arrays at runtime. To free memory occupied by arrays, use ERASE during program execution. Does not affect arrays that are not dimensioned with a DIM statement, which are always $STATIC. For more information, see discussion of arrays in "Programming Essentials" section.

# $INCLUDE

*Metacommand*

### Syntax

```
REM $INCLUDE: file
```

### Purpose

Instructs BASIC to include BASIC program lines in *file* specified within program at that point as if they were part of program. The *file* must be a BASIC source file. No SUB or FUNCTION statements may be included in an $INCLUDE file.

# $STATIC

*Metacommand*

### Syntax

```
REM $STATIC
```

### Purpose

Instructs BASIC to allocate memory for arrays during compilation. ERASE can set array values to zero (numeric) or null (string) but cannot free memory occupied by arrays. For more information, see discussion of arrays in "Programming Essentials" section.

# Reserved Words

The following list shows QuickBASIC 4.0 reserved
words. You cannot use any of these words as a variable,
label, or procedure name. Quick Library words, such as
ABSOLUTE and INTERRUPT, are excluded.

| | | |
|---|---|---|
| ABS | CONST | ERDEV$ |
| ACCESS | COS | ERL |
| ALIAS | CSNG | ERR |
| AND | CSRLIN | ERROR |
| ANY | CVD | EXIT |
| APPEND | CVDMBF | EXP |
| AS | CVI | FIELD |
| ASC | CVL | FILEATTR |
| ATN | CVS | FILES |
| BASE | CVSMBF | FIX |
| BEEP | DATA | FOR |
| BINARY | DATE$ | FRE |
| BLOAD | DECLARE | FREEFILE |
| BSAVE | DEF | FUNCTION |
| BYVAL | DEFDBL | GET |
| CALL | DEFINT | GOSUB |
| CALLS | DEFLNG | GOTO |
| CASE | DEFSNG | HEX$ |
| CDBL | DEFSTR | IF |
| CDECL | DIM | IMP |
| CHAIN | DO | INKEY$ |
| CHDIR | DOUBLE | INP |
| CHR$ | DRAW | INPUT |
| CINT | ELSE | INPUT$ |
| CIRCLE | ELSEIF | INSTR |
| CLEAR | END | INT |
| CLNG | ENDIF | INTEGER |
| CLOSE | ENVIRON | IOCTL |
| CLS | ENVIRON$ | IOCTL$ |
| COLOR | EOF | IS |
| COM | EQV | KEY |
| COMMAND$ | ERASE | KILL |
| COMMON | ERDEV | LBOUND |

| | | |
|---|---|---|
| LCASE$ | PEEK | SPACE$ |
| LEFT$ | PEN | SPC |
| LEN | PLAY | SQR |
| LET | PMAP | STATIC |
| LINE | POINT | STEP |
| LIST | POKE | STICK |
| LOC | POS | STOP |
| LOCAL | PRESET | STR$ |
| LOCATE | PRINT | STRIG |
| LOCK | PSET | STRING |
| LOF | PUT | STRING$ |
| LOG | RANDOM | SUB |
| LONG | RANDOMIZE | SWAP |
| LOOP | READ | SYSTEM |
| LPOS | REDIM | TAB |
| LPRINT | REM | TAN |
| LSET | RESET | THEN |
| LTRIM$ | RESTORE | TIME$ |
| MID$ | RESUME | TIMER |
| MKD$ | RETURN | TO |
| MKDIR | RIGHT$ | TROFF |
| MKDMBF$ | RMDIR | TRON |
| MKI$ | RND | TYPE |
| MKL$ | RSET | UBOUND |
| MKS$ | RTRIM$ | UCASE$ |
| MKSMBF$ | RUN | UNLOCK |
| MOD | SADD | UNTIL |
| NAME | SCREEN | USING |
| NEXT | SEEK | VAL |
| NOT | SEG | VARPTR |
| OCT$ | SELECT | VARPTR$ |
| OFF | SETMEM | VARSEG |
| ON | SGN | VIEW |
| OPEN | SHARED | WAIT |
| OPTION | SHELL | WEND |
| OR | SIGNAL | WHILE |
| OUT | SIN | WIDTH |
| OUTPUT | SINGLE | WINDOW |
| PAINT | SLEEP | WRITE |
| PALETTE | SOUND | XOR |
| PCOPY | | |

# Error Messages

QuickBASIC has many possible error messages. Most of them are self-explanatory, but many things may cause error messages. Only a quick listing of error messages is given here because a detailed explanation of each error is beyond the scope of this quick reference.

## *Invocation Errors*

The following errors may occur when you start Quick-BASIC with the qb command:

Cannot find file *filename*. Input path:

Error during QuickBASIC initialization

Error in loading file (*file*) – Cannot find file

Error in loading file (*file*) – Disk I/O error

Error in loading file (*file*) – DOS memory-arena error

Error in loading file (*file*) – Invalid format

Requires DOS 2.10 or later

Valid options: [RUN] file /AH /B /C:buf /G /H /L [lib] /MBF /CMD string

You may see the following errors when you invoke the compiler from the command line with the bc command:

Buffer size expected after /C:

/C: buffer size too large

Cannot generate listing for BASIC binary source files

Colon expected after /C

Extra file name ignored

Input file not found

Line invalid. Start again

Option unknown: *option*

Out of memory

Read error on standard input

# Compile-Time and QuickBASIC Environment Errors and Warnings

QuickBASIC generates the following errors and warnings when you are entering statements and Quick-BASIC checks the syntax, and when you are compiling a program from the command line with the **bc** command. The warnings, which do not suspend operation or compilation, indicate the existence of potential problems. Unless labeled as warnings, the following messages are errors:

Advanced feature unavailable

Argument count mismatch

Array already dimensioned

Array not defined

Array not dimensioned (Warning)

Array too big

AS clause required

AS clause required on first declaration

AS missing

Asterisk Missing

BASE missing

Binary source file

Block IF without END IF

BYVAL allowed only with numeric arguments

Cannot continue

Cannot start with 'FN'

CASE without SELECT

Choose New from Edit menu to create new SUB or function

Comma missing

COMMON and DECLARE must precede executable statements

COMMON in Quick library too small

COMMON name illegal

CONST/DIM SHARED follows SUB/FUNCTION (Warning)

Control structure in IF...THEN...ELSE incomplete

Data-memory overflow

DECLARE required

DEF FN not allowed in control statements

DEF without END DEF

DEF*type* character specification illegal

Division by zero

DO without LOOP

Document too large

Duplicate definition

Duplicate label

Dynamic array element illegal

Element not defined

ELSE without IF

ELSEIF without IF

END DEF without DEF

END IF without block IF

END SELECT without SELECT

END SUB or END FUNCTION must be last line in window

END SUB/FUNCTION without SUB/FUNCTION

END TYPE without TYPE

Equal sign missing

EXIT DO not within DO...LOOP

EXIT not within FOR...NEXT

Expected: *item*

Expression too complex

File previously loaded

Fixed-length string illegal

FOR index variable already in use

FOR index variable illegal

FOR without NEXT

Formal parameter specification illegal

Formal parameters not unique

Function already defined

Function name illegal

Function not defined

GOSUB missing

GOTO missing

GOTO or GOSUB expected

Identifier cannot end with %, &, !, #, or $

Identifier cannot include period

Identifier expected

Identifier too long

Illegal in direct mode

Illegal in procedure or DEF FN

Illegal number

Illegal outside of SUB, FUNCTION, or DEF FN

Illegal outside of SUB/FUNCTION

Illegal outside of TYPE block

Illegal type character in numeric constant

$INCLUDE-file access error

Include file too large

INPUT missing

Integer between 1 and 32767 required

Internal error near *xxxx*

Invalid character

Invalid constant

Invalid DECLARE for BASIC procedure

Label not defined

Label not defined: *label*

Left parenthesis missing

Line number or label missing

Line too long

LOOP without DO

Lower bound exceeds upper bound

Math overflow

$Metacommand error (Warning)

Minus sign missing

Missing Event Trapping (/W) or Checking Between
Statements (/V) option

Missing On Error (/E) option

Missing Resume Next (/X) option

Module level code too large

Module not found. Unload module from program?
(Warning)

Must be first statement on the line

Name of subprogram illegal

Nested function definition

NEXT missing for *variable*

NEXT without FOR

No main module. Choose Set Main Module from the
Run menu to select one

Numeric array illegal

Only simple variables allowed

Operation requires disk

Out of data space

Out of memory

Overflow in numeric constant

Parameter type mismatch

Procedure already defined in Quick library

Procedure too large

Program-memory overflow

Record/string assignment required

Right parenthesis missing

SEG or BYVAL not allowed in CALLS

SELECT without END SELECT

Semicolon missing

Separator illegal

Simple or array variable expected

Skipping forward to END TYPE statement

Statement cannot occur within $INCLUDE file

Statement cannot precede SUB/FUNCTION definition

Statement ignored (Warning)

Statement illegal in TYPE block

Statement unrecognizable

Statements/labels illegal between SELECT CASE and
    CASE

String assignment required

String constant required for ALIAS

String expression required

String variable required

SUB or FUNCTION missing

SUB/FUNCTION without END SUB/FUNCTION

Subprogram error

Subprogram not defined

Subprograms not allowed in control statements

Subscript syntax illegal

Syntax error

Syntax error in numeric constant

THEN missing

TO missing

Too many arguments in function call

Too many dimensions

Too many files

Too many labels

Too many named COMMON blocks

Too many TYPE definitions

Too many variables for INPUT

Too many variables for LINE INPUT

Type mismatch

Type missing

Type more than 65535 bytes

Type not defined

TYPE statement improperly nested

TYPE without END TYPE

Typed variable not allowed in expression

Unexpected end of file in TYPE declaration

Unrecognized switch error: "QU"

Variable length string required

Variable name not unique

Variable required

WEND without WHILE

WHILE without WEND

Wrong number of dimensions

# Run-Time Errors

The following errors can occur during program execution. When QuickBASIC gives an ERR code, that code is the numeric code returned by the ERR function in an error-handling routine. Some run-time errors are so severe that recovery is not possible; such errors are labeled here as NT (not trappable).

Two lists are provided. The first is sorted alphabetically, the second is sorted numerically.

| **Run-time error** | **ERR** |
| --- | --- |
| Advanced feature unavailable | 73 |
| Array already dimensioned | |
| Bad file mode | 54 |
| Bad file name | 64 |
| Bad file name or number | 52 |
| Bad record length | 59 |
| Bad record number | 63 |
| CASE ELSE expected | 39 |
| Communication-buffer overflow | 69 |
| Device fault | 25 |
| Device I/O error | 57 |
| Device timeout | 24 |
| Device unavailable | 68 |
| Disk full | 61 |
| Disk-media error | 72 |
| Disk not ready | 71 |
| Division by zero | 11 |
| Duplicate definition | 10 |
| Error in loading file (*file*) | |
| Out of memory | 7 |
| FIELD overflow | 50 |
| FIELD statement active | 56 |
| File already exists | 58 |
| File already open | 55 |
| File not found | 53 |
| Illegal function call | 5 |
| Input past end of file | 62 |
| Input runtime module path | NT |
| Internal error | 51 |
| No line number in *module-name* at address *segment:offset* | NT |
| No RESUME | 19 |
| Out of DATA | 4 |
| Out of data space | 7 |
| Out of memory | 7 |
| Out of paper | 27 |
| Out of stack space | NT |
| Out of string space | 14 |
| Overflow | 6 |
| Path not found | 76 |

| Path/File access error | 75 |
|---|---|
| Permission denied | 70 |
| Redo from start | |
| Rename across disks | 74 |
| Requires DOS 2.10 or later | |
| RESUME without error | 20 |
| RETURN without GOSUB | 3 |
| STOP in module *name* at address *segment:offset* | |
| String formula too complex | 16 |
| String space corrupt | |
| Subscript out of range | 9 |
| Syntax error | 2 |
| Too many files | 67 |
| Type mismatch | 13 |
| Unprintable error | |
| Variable required | 40 |

| **ERR** | **Run-time error** |
|---|---|
| 2 | Syntax error |
| 3 | RETURN without GOSUB |
| 4 | Out of DATA |
| 5 | Illegal function call |
| 6 | Overflow |
| 7 | Out of memory |
| 9 | Subscript out of range |
| 10 | Duplicate definition |
| 11 | Division by zero |
| 13 | Type mismatch |
| 14 | Out of string space |
| 16 | String formula too complex |
| 19 | No RESUME |
| 20 | RESUME without error |
| 24 | Device timeout |
| 25 | Device fault |
| 27 | Out of paper |
| 39 | CASE ELSE expected |
| 40 | Variable required |
| 50 | FIELD overflow |
| 51 | Internal error |
| 52 | Bad file name or number |
| 53 | File not found |
| 54 | Bad file mode |

| 55 | File already open |
| 56 | FIELD statement active |
| 57 | Device I/O error |
| 58 | File already exists |
| 59 | Bad record length |
| 61 | Disk full |
| 62 | Input past end of file |
| 63 | Bad record number |
| 64 | Bad file name |
| 67 | Too many files |
| 68 | Device unavailable |
| 69 | Communication-buffer overflow |
| 70 | Permission denied |
| 71 | Disk not ready |
| 72 | Disk-media error |
| 73 | Advanced feature unavailable |
| 74 | Rename across disks |
| 75 | Path/File access error |
| 76 | Path not found |

# Keyboard Codes

The following list shows the decimal values of the keyboard codes returned by each key and key combination. You may read these codes with the INKEY$ function. Note that certain keys and key combinations return two values in an extended code. For each of these extended codes, the first value returned is the null value, decimal value 0. Whenever the INKEY$ function returns a value of zero, the keyboard has returned an extended code. You should use the INKEY$ function a second time to obtain the second value.

| Key | Pressed Alone | With Shift | With Ctrl | With Alt |
|-----|------|------|------|------|
| A | 97 | 65 | 1 | 0 30 |
| B | 98 | 66 | 2 | 0 48 |
| C | 99 | 67 | 3 | 0 46 |
| D | 100 | 68 | 4 | 0 32 |
| E | 101 | 69 | 5 | 0 18 |
| F | 102 | 70 | 6 | 0 33 |

| Key | Pressed Alone | With Shift | With Ctrl | With Alt |
|-----|-----|-----|-----|-----|
| G | 103 | 71 | 7 | 0 34 |
| H | 104 | 72 | 8 | 0 35 |
| I | 105 | 73 | 9 | 0 23 |
| J | 106 | 74 | 10 | 0 36 |
| K | 107 | 75 | 11 | 0 37 |
| L | 108 | 76 | 12 | 0 38 |
| M | 109 | 77 | 13 | 0 50 |
| N | 110 | 78 | 14 | 0 49 |
| O | 111 | 79 | 15 | 0 24 |
| P | 112 | 80 | 16 | 0 25 |
| Q | 113 | 81 | 17 | 0 16 |
| R | 114 | 82 | 18 | 0 19 |
| S | 115 | 83 | 19 | 0 31 |
| T | 116 | 84 | 20 | 0 20 |
| U | 117 | 85 | 21 | 0 22 |
| V | 118 | 86 | 22 | 0 47 |
| W | 119 | 87 | 23 | 0 17 |
| X | 120 | 88 | 24 | 0 45 |
| Y | 121 | 89 | 25 | 0 21 |
| Z | 122 | 90 | 26 | 0 44 |
| 1 ! | 49 | 33 | -- | 0 120 |
| 2 @ | 50 | 64 | 0 3 | 0 121 |
| 3 # | 51 | 35 | -- | 0 122 |
| 4 $ | 52 | 36 | -- | 0 123 |
| 5 % | 53 | 37 | -- | 0 124 |
| 6 ^ | 54 | 94 | 30 | 0 125 |
| 7 & | 55 | 38 | -- | 0 126 |
| 8 * | 56 | 42 | -- | 0 127 |
| 9 ( | 57 | 40 | -- | 0 128 |
| 0 ) | 48 | 41 | -- | 0 129 |
| , < | 44 | 60 | -- | -- |
| . > | 46 | 62 | -- | -- |
| / ? | 47 | 63 | -- | -- |
| ; : | 59 | 58 | -- | -- |
| ' " | 39 | 34 | -- | -- |
| [ { | 91 | 123 | 27 | -- |
| ] } | 93 | 125 | 29 | -- |
| + _ | 45 | 95 | 31 | 0 130 |
| = + | 61 | 43 | -- | 0 131 |
| \ \| | 92 | 124 | 28 | -- |

| Key | Pressed Alone | With Shift | With Ctrl | With Alt |
|---|---|---|---|---|
| ` ~ | 96 | 126 | -- | -- |
| Enter | 13 | 13 | 10 | -- |
| Tab | 9 | 0  15 | -- | -- |
| Bksp | 8 | 8 | 127 | -- |
| Space | 32 | 32 | 32 | 32 |
| Esc | 27 | 27 | 27 | -- |
| * PrtScr | 42 | -- | 16 | -- |
| Home | 0  71 | 55 | 0  119 | -- |
| Up | 0  72 | 56 | -- | -- |
| PgUp | 0  73 | 57 | 0  132 | -- |
| Left | 0  75 | 52 | 0  115 | -- |
| Center | -- | 53 | -- | -- |
| Right | 0  77 | 54 | 0  116 | -- |
| End | 0  79 | 49 | 0  117 | -- |
| Down | 0  80 | 50 | -- | -- |
| PgDn | 0  81 | 51 | 0  118 | -- |
| Ins | 0  82 | 48 | -- | -- |
| Del | 0  83 | 46 | -- | -- |
| Grey + | 43 | 43 | -- | -- |
| Grey + | 45 | 45 | -- | -- |
| F1 | 0  59 | 0  84 | 0  94 | 0  104 |
| F2 | 0  60 | 0  85 | 0  95 | 0  105 |
| F3 | 0  61 | 0  86 | 0  96 | 0  106 |
| F4 | 0  62 | 0  87 | 0  97 | 0  107 |
| F5 | 0  63 | 0  88 | 0  98 | 0  108 |
| F6 | 0  64 | 0  89 | 0  99 | 0  109 |
| F7 | 0  65 | 0  90 | 0  100 | 0  110 |
| F8 | 0  66 | 0  91 | 0  101 | 0  111 |
| F9 | 0  67 | 0  92 | 0  102 | 0  112 |
| F10 | 0  68 | 0  93 | 0  103 | 0  113 |

# Index